FIND WORLDWIDE PEACE

FIND WORLDWIDE PEACE

MARK STEVEN BARTLETT

International Edition
Published 2025
by Mark Steven Bartlett

ISBN 978-0-473-76512-5 (international edition)

ISBN 978-0-473-76510-1 (Paperback)

ISBN 978-0-473-76511-8 (Epub)

© Copyright Mark Steven Bartlett 2025

All rights reserved.

Except for the purpose of fair reviewing, no part of this publication may be reproduced or transmitted in any form or by any means, electronic or mechanical, including photocopying, recording or any information storage and retrieval system, without prior written permission from the publisher.

COPYPRESS

Designed and distributed in New Zealand by
CopyPress, Nelson, New Zealand.

www.copypress.co.nz

CONTENTS

Chapter 1:	THE PERFECT KEY		1
Chapter 2:	FAMILIES AND COMMUNITIES		14
Chapter 3:	GOVERNMENTS		29
Chapter 4:	WORLD ECONOMY		43
Chapter 5:	A NEW EDUCATION		51
Chapter 6:	RELIGIONS TRANSFORM		63
Chapter 7:	LADDERS INTO SPIRITUALITY		73
Chapter 8:	GENDER, SEXISM AND HOMOPHOBIA		86
Chapter 9:	POVERTY, POLLUTION AND DISEASE		92
Chapter 10:	NATURAL DISASTERS		97
Chapter 11:	RACE AND CULTURE		104
Chapter 12:	NATIONALISM AND XENOPHOBIA		113
Chapter 13:	WAR, PEACE AND JUSTICE		120

Chapter 14:	**DEFEAT VICTORY**	131
Chapter 15:	**TIME AND MATTER**	142
Chapter 16:	**AN INDIVIDUALITY CONNECTION**	149
Chapter 17:	**CRIME AND MERCY**	160
Chapter 18:	**TEARS AND LAUGHTER**	169
Chapter 19:	**AGEING WITH JOY**	177
Chapter 20:	**MINDFULNESS**	185
Chapter 21:	**THE ARRIVAL**	195

ABOUT THE AUTHOR

The author, Mark Steven Bartlett, has written his first book 'Find Worldwide Peace'. He has had a lifelong interest in peace, beginning as a child wishing for peace in his home life, and then, as an adult, noticing the harm and destruction in the world, he developed a passion for world peace. He feels that it is part of his essence to write this book. His hope is that it may help others to find worldwide peace, by touching on every topic necessary for peace and explaining it, and by transferring the thoughts and messages from his intuition into a conventional format that people will be able to understand. He lives in Nelson, New Zealand.

CHAPTER 1

THE PERFECT KEY

The key is one thing that will find worldwide peace.

Envisage a real key that is unlocking the secrets and opening the doors to world peace.

I will take you into each different subject that is an obstacle to peace, and each chapter will touch on an area that needs to change.

There is a puzzle that needs to be put together in people's minds. Each chapter contains a piece of the puzzle that needs to be connected to the other pieces to make a completed full puzzle. Read all the chapters and put the pieces together to know all that is required to have peace.

Current established institutions, systems and attitudes have to go, and transformation is necessary to replace the old ways that are ingrained in us. From reading this book you will know what has to be done to replace the old with the new. Then, in time, when the portal opens into the Age of Aquarius, we will be in alignment with it and will go through the portal in an automatic flow.

We want to shout from the mountaintops to sound an alarm that will awaken people to what needs to be done, to eliminate the bad and lift up humanity to the greatest heights of achievement that they can attain, by using the key given in this book. We shout from the mountaintops to all people everywhere to heed our call for peace worldwide. People will listen when they hear us as they know the echoes of voices from the mountaintops are the wake-up call for all of humanity.

This will be an exciting time as universal portals will be opening, and we will understand the alignment with oneness energy that we will be working with. Collaboration between humans is wise, and with everyone's support and combining of ideas we will go into the portal for Aquarius.

The time zone of the fifth dimension will be occupied by everybody as the following chapters of this book will explain.

This book describes the difficult process necessary to transform into a new reality. I have written this book and have put these chapters together as I know the process that is required to be done to transform the obstacles. Unfolding throughout this book and shown in every chapter is the action needed for people to let go of old beliefs and move on into new age understanding. It will make people rethink all issues about the way the world is. They will discuss it with their peers, and it may open their minds to new ideas and possibilities which may give people hope for a better world in the future.

Organising and decision-making is agonising for people, but reading the chapters of this book will reveal the outcome to them so they can be stress-free. It is set out clearly in a conventional way that relies on the process of actions and changes to accomplish the outcome, to give the reader the realisation and knowing of how to find world peace.

A forgiving and caring attitude is necessary for people with different beliefs to cooperate with one another toward common goals. We need to understand the key connection between the material world and the spiritual world to maintain our wellbeing. The key connection is the law of cause and effect, which is that what we do to others comes back to us.

The universe is preparing us for what we need to do and is automatically supporting us with a new frequency of energy, which gives us the courage to speak up about the new information. Some people may begin thinking for themselves just from reading this book.

Concerns about ongoing wars on Earth cause people to think that things are getting worse in the world, especially with the news media showing extensive dramatic coverage of wars. There is just a lot of confusion in people's minds which makes it seem like things are getting worse, but they are actually getting better. The actual outcomes of wars on Earth may not be good or bad, as it depends which side of the war you are on as to whether you think the outcome is good or bad. Revenge or forgiveness also is not good or bad, as those on one side of the war may think that revenge is good and is the right action to take, and those on the other side may believe that forgiveness is good and what they should do, therefore it depends on your point of view. Karmically if something is meant to happen there is nothing bad about it. As we are currently at the crossroads, the fulfilment of events has to happen as they are supposed to.

Contemplation must be done by humans on how to end wars and live peacefully.

The darkest hour is increasing the confusion, as we cannot understand why things are getting worse when they are supposed to be getting better. The universe has no emotions and supports us in whatever we want and put forth; for example, if we want war, the universe supports war. When things get so bad that we will start getting our act together, then the confusion of the darkest hour will be dissolved by the light of Aquarius, (the new age), which will start resolving things for inner peace and peace out in the world to ensue.

Forming strategies to confront what is exposed; the wars, conflicts, poverty, disease and phobias, is vital. Good people must overpower bad people so that anything in the control of the bad people must change to the control of the good people. Strategies need to be worked out in detail and have stages, one step at a time, to keep them better organised and accurate, and more likely to get the desired results. You have to work it out step by step, and the universe that supports you 100% automatically supports your organising as long as you go with the flow of what happens.

The key point of this book is to show promising data in the information presented by the explanations in each chapter, that will achieve our goal of working together cooperatively.

All calls from the mountaintops are the universe supporting people to work together to change the programming, using their new understanding. Those people who are doing the reprogramming need to specify the details to avoid any confusion. When confusion is removed you can think clearly about the outcome, which leads to the perfect conclusion and a specific program to live by.

There could be community conferences to work out ways of eliminating confusion. The more government and community conferences that take place, the more confusion will be cleared. Until confusion is removed, we cannot progress, as it is too hard to live the new life with confusion in our minds.

There is a lot of controversy about new age beliefs. Some people are very ingrained in their religion, and there is so much confusion in the world and in people's minds. Until it is dissolved, they cannot be programmed with the new frequency of the universe and with the ideas of the new state of spirituality, from the new era.

For worldwide peace to even be possible, we all need to reach inner peace within ourselves, with our mind, body and spirit being fully united. This will be possible, and what you will ideally need to achieve this will be explained as you continue reading this book. The elimination of all confusion will turn things around in people's thinking, also in what they are doing, and what they are receiving in new skills, to develop the new age of caring and sharing the abundance fairly.

Once we get confusion out of the way, (as confusion is terrible), we can see clearly what is ahead. It opens people up to new ways of thinking and taking notice of new age skills. Things that were previously confused will now be identified clearly. There will be many advantages of clearing the confusion, and it will advance the movement forward. When confusion is gone we can make final plans about what our aims are, which will include everybody.

Ingrained beliefs that some people have makes them unable to accept new age beliefs. It is what is ingrained in people that is holding them back. Some people cannot change no matter what they are being told, and this allows them to drop back. Dimensional reality is confusing for those who do not understand.

Many people will continue debating, as they do not feel a connection to the new age information. The religious people that are so ingrained will be the last ones to follow on and accept new ideas and change. They will still think the new age is 'airy-fairy', as their religious teachings have been so strong, and for such a long time. Religious people will at least take notice of what is outside their religion and may be curious about the new age and may want to make enquiries about it.

When we see proof of the afterlife and of the spiritual realm that we will understand, we will see it in a whole new way. To prove the spiritual realm through computer programming is what has to be done, for people to interact in a new age manner to fulfil Earth's destiny of peace.

All have wanted world peace for so long, but they have to understand that confusion is at a crossroads with the disruption it causes. This will be followed by gains through interacting with one another in community conferences, by gathering a large amount of information and combining it into a whole. Strong agreements must be made in these community conferences and an understanding gained of how to support the government and persuade it to make big changes. All the communities will connect and contribute on a large scale with huge support for a new mindset amongst everyone in society.

When the dawn arises, after the darkest hour, the confusion will fade away. During the darkest hour we have to work around the confusion; with the dawn the confusion automatically fades.

There are bad people and good people on this Earth, and they all want to behave in the way that fits into their lifestyle and way of thinking. This is an example of confusion in the third dimension and crossroads, as they are all going their own way with no understanding or interest in the new beliefs that need to be incorporated into everyone.

People will rethink things when the universe supports us into the fifth dimension, and new age beliefs are interpreted to show them there is a whole new way to world peace. For example, religious people think that if everyone joins their religion, everyone will be 'saved', and world peace will be here. When the new age comes in, religious people will be able to use their sixth sense to follow the new spirituality. They will be able to break their ingrained beliefs because they will have happiness in their hearts, as they realise there is a new way to go to have peace in the world. Everyone will feel the happiness in their heart. Spiritual and religious people will go equally into the new age. Those who are religious will see the future ahead of them when they no longer have confusion; they will then understand the spiritualist beliefs.

Proof of the afterlife/heaven will have to arrive before strongly religious citizens can manage to turn their lives around. This will happen when science and spirituality together will prove the afterlife exists. Other things will help and support this, such as the understanding of the information in this book. When there is proof of the afterlife, people will KNOW what the afterlife is like and will KNOW the universe. This will be enforced by universal laws coming through noticeably to the Earth, in the form of new vibrational energy.

Governments will be capable of writing documents that incorporate spirituality. We must begin living by the universal law of cause and effect, and the public must be informed of this.

Religious believers will realise that they will have to step out of their religion to see the right course of action for themselves. The only way they will achieve the understanding to move into world peace is by moving out of their religion.

World peace requirements will need to be looked into by governments who will have contact with extraterrestrials. Governments will confide in each other about the things the extraterrestrials tell them, but keep these things secret from the public as the information is not conventional and the public would not accept it at this stage. Extraterrestrials keep in contact with governments and tell them what is needed to be done and how to organise a new reality.

The universe, in giving back to us what we have put out, is informing and supplying us with its forceful energy. It is at the fourth-dimensional crossroads of putting all the dynamics, the energetic parts, together so they connect. When confusion is dissolved, everything will come together and work well. The dynamics will create such a rapid domino effect that it will really get the job done at a faster rate automatically, to connect the puzzle for world peace.

All of the good news about what is happening and being sorted out in the world will be covered by the news media. Everyone, the public and the government, will agree and will be interested and informed in hearing such positive news, as they all want peace in the world.

The higher energy of Aquarius will start the healing of karma from the Piscean age; the negativity from wars and male dominance over the last 2000 years. When we can prove the spiritual world exists, everything, being the communities, governments, the universe and spirits in heaven, will be integrated in a domino chain reaction effect.

After the government or a highly evolved scientist has given proof of the afterlife, then official government diplomats will share the information. They will make speeches about the essential steps to be done, in order to get things right for the public so they will know how to work together. They will give talks on how to do things and how to put the new spirituality into place. The new unconventional information will stir things up quite a bit in the communities. Things are changing for them, and they are not used to it, or they cannot adjust. Diplomats will become more evolved and stronger with more understanding of spirituality. We will keep becoming more evolved with science and spirituality, and this does away with third-dimensional reality that we now look back on as being stupid and unaware and lower consciousness.

A forum can be held to bring the public together for open discussion and debate on how to have control with an even outcome, on spirituality. This is inspired by intelligent people so they can perform by sharing the information around, to help out the rest of the community.

The introverted personalities of some individuals hold them back from communicating, but they will be supported by those who are extroverted and who can help them to communicate and keep them fully informed in the community gatherings. Communities will do whatever it takes to support everyone in their community to attain fifth-dimensional reality.

We will all be able to move into one timeline together. What we accomplish with everyone, with our healing abilities and scientific proof of spirituality, will enable us to move everyone into the same timeline, all living in the new age. There are different timelines on Earth in our spiritual reality, and we will identify these timelines so that we can work to move us all into one timeline.

When we are all doing this work together, we are fully connected in oneness, and this gives us 100% power to be successful.

Forgiveness is important for all issues, for the harm that anyone has done, from war, family issues, conflicts, and all deep overwhelming issues that are heartbreaking.

You need to keep thinking and reading about the procedure to move ahead; what your next steps should be, and what you need to do to meet up, and align with, one timeline for us all, being in fifth-dimensional reality.

We will really notice the fifth-dimensional reality; the light coming through strongly with love.

Third-dimensional reality, which for us is normal daily life, by transforming into fifth-dimensional reality, is like the beginning of the rebirth of a new civilisation. We will be moving into fifth-dimensional reality and have proof of the spiritual world here in the physical world. We will adjust to being free from confusion and having enhanced lives because of the convergence between the two worlds.

Two things are needed to reach our goal (of the fifth dimension); the awakening of the population, and the information they need.

Not only do we have an individual purpose for our own life, we also have the universal purpose in each one of us to work with the rest of the human population to reach our highest goals. We know we have a connection of oneness with all other people, and we need to connect together at all times. This will create the circumstance of full universal reflection, whereby the universe will reflect back the oneness that will go on to create peace.

Clear words and actions from the government and community leaders to the public will activate a thorough fifth-dimensional alignment in the minds of the listeners. The new universal order of getting together for peace will bring out the best behaviour from the highest people in power, and from light workers, spiritual leaders and all those that are working for good in society.

All religion in the material world is dropping out, so people are then connecting with spirituality and the spiritual world.

Automatic upheaval in all societies will occur as they make changes from their ordinary conventional way of living, empowered by their top leaders. This increases people's living in the mindset of getting things right in every way in the present moment, to be uplifted for a better brighter future. Spiritual leaders in the community will orientate people on what to do and where to go, to center them and organise them into fifth-dimensional spirituality.

The extreme force of our thoughts is the extreme force of the universe as they are 100% connected. We really need to notice our thoughts carefully. However, once we are in the fifth dimension our thoughts will be ingrained into place, into living and working in that reality of a higher enlightenment, and all negative thoughts will fade out.

Knowing inner peace and working together to know world peace to its full extent, and to see what is needed for peace, will give us the outcome that we want. Living and working by rules that apply to everyone globally, that have been made by governments and authorities influenced and guided by the higher light, the higher frequency of energy and higher awareness, fills us all with joy. Our material world practices will be strongly influenced by the intervention of the spiritual world for the benefit of our wellbeing.

Universal laws, such as the law of oneness and the law of cause and effect, will be made widely known in society, along with the encouragement of positive companionship, friendship and harmony amongst the population, to enhance their lives and give them support. Positivity in the news media will reassure them and give them confidence.

From the new age heart, where humans will think and feel in the new way in their hearts, will come the birth of the new age, and the realisation that to be better off there must be certain standards that are adhered to by those in authority, so that they use their power wisely and for the betterment of all. Sometimes when those in power have too much power, they can abuse it.

Our way of thinking will be changed by the energy frequency and by the order, structure and makeup of the universe, and by governments. With our new thoughts we will automatically go into the new age.

We all need to come into the fifth dimension. We have to drop out of third-dimensional ingrained thinking so that it is possible for us to be realigned for the fifth dimension, and to enhance our knowledge within the energy framework of the fifth dimension.

We have to learn to communicate with the third-dimensional people that were falling behind, so that they will socially accept others who are different from them. Those third-dimensional people will learn from the leaders to have a new interpretation of what they are realising about the new age, which will take them to the fifth dimension. The purpose of their education is important; it is meant for everyone to go into fifth-dimensional reality. My writing in this book will resemble what the leaders teach about the new age.

Wishful thinking about going into the fifth dimension keeps us on the right track and keeps us moving toward it. Knowing you are on the right track is exciting, because you can see what is ahead in the golden era, that will be a celebration for everybody.

We will feel magnificent achievement within ourselves when we reach the landmark of the fifth dimension with the support of the universe, having kicked all of the bad out of the way, and we enter fifth-dimensional spirituality with excitement and the prospect of peace. Excitement is the emotion that goes with the perfect key, as excitement builds momentum and energy and the feeling that it is all working out perfectly.

The principle behind the perfect key is noticing your own inner peace to find what is right for worldwide peace. That is a promise, as all peace that is within us comes out of us.

CHAPTER 2

FAMILIES AND COMMUNITIES

You are brought into this world by your parents, who bring you up in the way that they want to. This can seem very controlling to children, and the attitudes, beliefs and behaviours of your mother and father have an important effect on you when your young brain is developing. You may also have brothers and/or sisters who may be older or younger than you, or your twin. They play a very significant part in your life, as you have to live in the same house together, and you may or may not get along with them. You learn things from your siblings as well as from your parents about family life interaction, coping with your family members and about following the household rules. Your life with your family will teach you the things you need to know for coping with adult life when you grow up and are managing life on your own. Even after you are an adult, you still have contact with your parents and siblings, and your relationship with them may be a bit different from when you were a child, but they will still play a significant role in your life.

When you are brought into this world, no matter how your parents treat you, you will still be reliant on them to look after you, and you will feel grief and longing for them and miss them when you are away from them, or if you do not feel emotionally supported by them, just because they are your parents and you feel a deep attachment to them. I know this for a fact from my personal experience in my own life from my parents. My parents seemed very different from each other. My father was mentally ill, and I was physically abused by him, but I still always felt grief whenever I was away from him. It is natural to feel this way, and you will find that you will feel the same about your parents, as you rely on them and they have such a major impact on your life. It is interesting to look back on your upbringing and see the phenomenal effect your parents had on you that resulted in who you are now.

When you are a child growing up, you notice how you are treated, and this teaches you a lot about people and about life. When you are an adult you use the knowledge learnt from your parents to make a life for yourself in this world. It helps you know what to do and where to go. You build up trust in yourself as a result of your upbringing, so that you can make gains in your life and enjoy the company of your friends. As life goes on you meet more and more friends and acquaintances and enjoy social contact and interaction that is beneficial. Talking things over and coming to agreements will help to keep friendships, as long as your friends also want to sort out differences of opinion.

There is a connection between our mind, body and spirit, but people doubt this and see these as being separate. This causes a lack of caring for others, and although some people are generous and kind-hearted, more often people are greedy and selfish and have no caring.

In small communities and townships, the locals tend to know each other better and are more friendly and perhaps more interested in helping others in their community. Local officials who have some power, and who want to use their power to help their community, as opposed to being corrupt and using their power for their own self-gain, can help the townspeople understand that they will all be better off if they unite. The officials can hand out brochures, knock on resident's doors to inform them, hold community meetings and make speeches, and run classes to assist the public to be helpful and friendly to each other.

They must follow the laws and rules of the locality and the country and not commit crimes, or they will suffer the consequences. Niceness and friendliness are the objective in their daily lives. Medical help for those taking drugs and abusing alcohol would be available. Behaviours can change in communities, as the good work, supportiveness and good behaviour of most townspeople can prevent bad deeds being done, when those who would do them are lifted up by the good vibes in the community. Small communities in society tend to grow and increase their population, and the good behaviours can still continue the same, with the community members following the rules and helping others and including the newcomers in the community.

To become a disciplined society is the ideal goal. Locals who are in positions of power need to create programs in the community, to make citizens aware of the need for self-discipline, to adhere to laws and local rules. Governments and local authorities use their power to keep order in society.

Those stubbornly resistant people who do not want to change will find themselves held back from moving forward with everyone else for world peace. But, as I have explained, with a lot of motivational support from the good people in their community, particularly those in positions of local power, the unimaginable happens, and those who did not previously want to change now want to be their best self and move to the other side of the bridge, to fifth-dimensional spirituality. The reason I say this is because clearly whenever you come upon a river and there is a bridge, it is so much easier to get to the other side of the river by crossing the bridge, and then you can keep moving along strongly with other people.

There is a strong sense in people's gut feelings that ignites in them the knowing to go on the right pathway, and they see how easy it is to come together with the knowledge they have.

Like turning on the ignition in a car, we can recognise how to ignite the motivation in those reluctant to change because they are so used to their old way of thinking. Proof of spirituality and the afterlife is needed before there will be world peace. Some people are so ingrained in old ways of thinking that they cannot adapt. The existence of the afterlife, and that life is eternal, will be proven by science and computer technology, which will lead to higher spirituality that makes us more evolved.

This will be beneficial to our brain cells, which will connect with each other more and more until they are all fully connected.

Progress will be made when there are documents showing proof of the afterlife. There will always be people who deny the proof; they have doubts, and they mistrust it. When we prove that the afterlife exists, there will be an increase in spirituality in society with many people seeking information about it. This information will be new, reliable and understandable, and will bring enjoyment and enhancement as well as coming together of people. All requests for information will result in excitement, upliftment and joy, and benefits for all inquirers.

The combination of all these events; the uniting of families and communities, the support from local authorities and officials, the programs and documents showing proof of the true reality, and communication to everyone so that the best that can happen does happen, results in the atmosphere and vibration being positive and high. Positive and competent behaviour by the citizens to get things right will deeply embed the benefits in the community.

The bonus effect of everyone coming together is that there is a more positive flow of events, and greater acceptance of each other. The new energy of the new age coming in creates a relaxed atmosphere you can adjust to that is more accepting.

When natural disasters happen there is kindness shown to those affected, because of the disruption to their lives and the losses they suffer. This reinforces to us that we should be kind to others at all times, not just in emergencies. Natural disasters wake us up, and they keep happening, to make us realise that we need to keep being kind and come together forever.

Local authorities and highly trusted professional people with high status in the community can increase the energy they already have, by uplifting the energy within themselves. This gives them a higher level of support and power from the universe, as all energy is connected, and there will be more interaction between the authorities and the citizens. Developing support amongst everyone maintains evenness, so that everyone is treated evenly and the same, and the higher level of energy and support brings peace.

As some communities begin to make these improvements, other communities see what they are doing and become aware of the advantages, and it encourages them to develop as well. People from some communities may visit these progressive communities and get good ideas from them to take back to their own community to implement. In this way communities help each other along.

Community programs that are all-inclusive and are administered efficiently, with good management and high spiritual ideals, will help everything flow to make life easier for the residents.

The work in communities that some people do to bring people together, such as spiritual teaching, may not be getting paid fairly, causing discontentment. As we move more into fifth-dimensional spirituality and become fully aligned with it, people will be paid fairly and have a clear understanding of spirituality. Many issues will no longer be a concern as everyone receives their fair share of pay. Those who combine working with the community with their spiritual teachings are accomplishing their purpose of coming into the new age.

Family and community are joining together with spirituality to bring us wellbeing in our lives and bring us together as one, by giving us information about what is best for our wellbeing. The atmospheric energy of the physical Earth in the outside world delivers a forceful positive change in energy, that we will feel and notice and comment on, to our friends and family.

It is certain that a small community in the richer countries of the developed world will begin the changes. Other communities will be interested and intrigued by what they see happening and they will start to follow the lead of the first small community, so that a much larger and growing number of communities change. Eventually this will spread to the poorer countries of the world.

The strong spiritual energy results in the equalising of gender entitlements so that women will receive equal and fair pay for their work. This equality of income, with men and women receiving even amounts, reunites everyone together; men, women and children, encompassing the whole family, with the income from both parents. The more we move into the fifth dimension, the more we will gather together in increasingly larger numbers, and the more equality of income there will be.

Our understanding of our world and our reality has been closed off by confusion, but now what was closed off is open again, giving us increased clarity, so that we can understand what we are capable of. Everything we understand depends on coming together in companionship. However, we are reluctant to change our familiar ways.

When we begin receiving the flow of energy from the universe, then we keep receiving more and more, and the flow is continual. Without us realising it, we automatically move into the fifth dimension. This happens naturally, without us intending it, and without our knowing.

It is important not to be reluctant to open up to change, but to welcome assertive expansion of coordinated growth, with the agreement of those who wish to cooperate in making steady movement forward.

Those who are keen and determined to change will be facing the opposition of those who are stuck in their ways and who want to stay in the third dimension. However, the push and drive of those making changes will sweep the naysayers along with them, as the momentum will be overpowering, and the effect will be that they will be pulled along with it, as the preferred outcome is change.

The changes will be agonising for many as they will find it difficult to adjust to coming together and working together with others.

The purpose of people congregating together is to benefit them all with uplifted high vibration energy, that uplifts our thinking in line with universal energy, which is very educational energy. This helps to clear our exasperated thinking and confusion. Because of confused thinking we have missed out on agreements and moving ahead at a faster rate.

Life cannot exist on Earth without water. We need good quality drinking water that must be clean and containable. Higher energy purifies the water and makes it more beneficial for our bodies. There will be enough water for everyone on Earth worldwide, but assertive behaviour is needed to ensure that water is shared and provided fairly to everyone.

Our thoughts about ourselves are also affected by higher energy. It makes our thoughts more positive, as we need to like and love ourselves more. People should talk nicely to each other and give each other compliments. Living in your community and complying with its standard equal behaviours, and living right, has consequences that are loving and better off in a much happier lifestyle.

So far in this chapter I have covered many things relating to families and communities. I have written about the gathering together of citizens in fifth-dimensional living, caring for each other more and having positive forward-thinking leaders to teach and preach about changes.

Many world leaders and activists are trying to get peace in the world and are trying to negotiate ceasefires and peace agreements between countries that are at war with each other. Different communities within the same country are sometimes also at war with each other, fighting for power, recognition, or human rights. Nations that have nuclear capability have refrained from using their nuclear weapons and this has averted worldwide nuclear catastrophe. A lot of diplomacy takes place constantly, with groups of countries meeting regularly to cooperate on issues, and to make agreements with mutual goals for the good of the planet and for peace. Even when ceasefires are broken and fighting resumes, the peace-seeking world leaders and diplomats continue trying to find peaceful solutions, and encourage the leaders of the conflicts to come to neutral locations or countries for peace talks, to try to resolve their disputes.

A peaceful future that once seemed so distant, because of the reluctance to change, now seems much nearer and more attainable. People notice the new frequency, the new awareness and the new order, the knowing of right and wrong and the combining for world peace.

There will be cures for health issues such as mental illness that would otherwise prevent those affected from following on.

Those who are reluctant and are lagging behind may need to be provoked to adapt and keep up. People are powerful; the reluctant ones will give in and go along with the flow, similar to a domino effect, and they will be productive as they will exploit the advantage this domino effect gives them to catch up to, and even up with, those ahead of them.

When the fog of confused thinking clears so that we can see the future, it is like going to sleep in the evening after twilight and waking at sunrise to a whole new world. From when you awake and get up at dawn, you have a hard-working day of achievement and financial benefit from helping others.

An energy uplift will shift old behavioural patterns to the frequency of the fifth dimension. The companionship of people gathering in friendliness enhances their wellbeing to do their jobs, and it is expected of them that they will do their duty to form and implement a complete plan for the benefit of their community.

The universe provides us with its high-quality energy that brings awareness to our consciousness. Being thankful for what we know and for the achievements from the shifts in attitudes and behaviours in our communities is a worthwhile attitude to have. Communities at large will transform behavioural patterns by teaching about the new energies.

Neighbourhood communities will know about the new consciousness and will grow from being small and separate into much larger developed societies. They will be uplifted in energy from all the spiritual preaching and teaching, causing people to choose the new spiritual beliefs. Spirituality will be understood in a whole new way, like moving into the new fifth-dimensional era in their mind. There will be more balance, fairness and understanding in them, because of this integration of the upliftment of energy and the new beliefs, which connects and combines into one whole in their mind.

The flow of the new energy is positive and inspiring, and also pleasant and desirable. The new way of understanding is positive and will be easily comprehended as it is what we instinctively know is true. The old way of understanding is negative and will not last.

Realignment of our thoughts and our energy with new ideas will make citizens more compassionate, and they will do the duties they have to do using the new knowledge, which will support them to be honest in their jobs and voluntary work. Thinking minds can enhance their duties by communicating and cooperating with compassion, with other residents in the community. Using the new knowledge, they will see the whole of everything, and they will know what to do.

Communication skills are a very important aspect of life. When individuals isolate themselves from society they miss out on socialising and communicating, and they do not know how to do these things. When they have been isolated for a long time it becomes a habit, and they are then afraid to go back into the community to socialise again, so they stay isolated out of fear. It can feel weird to go back out into a community again to mix with others. It takes a lot of adjusting to, and they would be lacking in confidence and social skills. Doing things together with others in the community takes effort, but when natural disasters occur it is forced upon us to help each other in communities.

Disastrous earthquakes rouse citizens to get out and help others who have been affected. The shaking of the Earth can cause a lot of destruction and results in an outpouring of help from the communities. Other major disasters such as fires and floods bring communities together to help each other and clean up the mess. The more resources of money and support services that are needed, and that citizens are entitled to, the more it makes helpers work together to assist in the best way that they can.

The supplies and resources provided when a natural disaster occurs must be of the highest standard. Discussions must take place in communities about the best way to get high quality support services, and about what is needed to bring all communities together. There is a mind frame about helping others; people have to get into a mind frame of helping.

The more I write about this, the more it will help you know these things. My explanations are the starting point to living a new reality as I am describing in this book. It is the way to live.

Behavioural human consciousness with communication and socialisation is important, to be aware of how we interact with one another. The way your mind thinks is what creates your behaviour. A new pattern is beginning now within all beings of human consciousness, that enhances the interactions between people relating to the discussion of facts, to know what is factual, and to know what matters.

The realignment of the planets, which causes new universal energy and order, brings a new vibration to our way of thinking. All of the discussions about the realignment of the new age and new thought must be done respectfully, using the accepted facts, while aspiring to increased wellbeing.

Your utmost highest thought is that which motivates you and fills your body with the energy you need, to do what is truly essential and what you intend to do. This makes you the way you are, and the more you keep walking right on ahead, the more you realise the mind, body and spirit connection. Ingrained in your consciousness is a stream that is in flow with your life as it happens.

We are living in a stronger awareness all the time, and moving with energised motion toward the fifth dimension, and we are doing this constantly, as the upward moving energy is always with us and is never-ending. Subconsciously we are aware of this energy, but we do not consciously know it, so it is missing in our consciousness. Our brain cells are not connected or evolved enough for fifth-dimensional reality. They need to evolve and connect with the ongoing reality that we are going to be moving into. This energy power will be incorporated right through us, and we will know how to use it correctly. The promise with this energy power is that what we believe, we know that we will receive it.

It is noticeable how people behave and react to others. They have to come to terms with the mixture of their reactions and emotions and their confusion, and also how to fit these in together with mind, body and spirit, and try to integrate them into the new world.

Receiving what you believe is enjoyable and removes your concerns so that you know you are in the fifth-dimensional world.

The growth of connections between communities is enjoyable when larger communities support smaller ones by giving them educational resources. The consequence of this supply of resources is the embracing of what has been given with kindness, and the feeling of being supported and feeling closer to the larger communities. I think the consequences of all this upheaval will be outstanding. Everything that is being taught, which is the informational resources from the highest spiritual leaders, will be grouped together and sent out to all the communities, to be equally fair to them all, and to advance the abundance, positivity and feeling of companionship that they gain from sharing. The effects of positive and negative behaviours and reactions will be communicated, with the information that the positive overrides the negative, so that the negative is reduced, and we can be living with good behaviour which strengthens the movement towards world peace.

The spiritual leaders are creating a trend of everyone coming together. The flow of the trend makes people want to join in and follow it. In this way, the spiritual leaders are using this flow to increase the numbers who follow this trend in behavioural patterns. The more positive we all are, and the more we connect, the more it increases our trust and certainty to do what we need to do and use our knowingness in every aspect of our lives.

We need to have an expectation of consideration and cooperation in our families and communities to create a caring society. People grow stronger knowing the facts that we can live by in our mind, and this causes our bodies to become stronger also. When we work hard together with all others in society the consequences have a positive effect on us all, and from the positive support we have given to others, we receive 100% support in return.

The spirit world observes what is happening and sees the conscientious programs of people working together on how life is meant to be. The high command in the spirit world is letting climate change happen on Earth so that we will reprogram our thoughts and think differently. Prominent people on Earth who have power will help other people to achieve things safely and positively.

What begins as a fraction of togetherness and realignment soon becomes much larger than just a fraction and then connects together as a complete whole. The written information has been supplied to all the communities for them to progress responsibly and reliably. Certainty, reliability and trustworthiness are the qualities necessary in communities to perform positive outcomes.

What we send out with our thoughts, the universe rebounds back to us 100%, so that the consequences of our thoughts affect us. Alignment in people's minds helps them progress in their understanding of the universe, and to realise their connection to it. This results in new learning and faster redevelopment through teamwork, and this means an uplift to world peace. Looking back, we can see that separation resulted in more negative viewpoints.

Once we are aligned in our heads we can move into the new Age of Aquarius, as we realise the new development of realignments and connection. By working in together we can understand the opening of the portal, so that we can move into the new age with a sense of excitement.

There is only one present, and being in the present moment and focusing on what we are doing right now in each moment is the best thing to do, whilst at the same time looking forward to a positive future, as we grasp and hold onto a vision of wellbeing and love as we all come together and work collectively. Realigning positive ideas and drafting out precise knowledge helps our communities to connect and communicate wisely and competently with flexibility. The forthright knowledge circulates around all the communities. Putting the teamwork in place to grow so that we are wise and sharing in our communities helps towards world peace.

The ignition (as in a vehicle) from turning the key on, enhances the unity of people working together, and when we are wise it means we can motor along to come together like a brotherhood. The motor signals we have to process regarding what is right when working together helps us to know exactly what has to be done. This enhances the non-stoppable abundant process to give us inner peace.

Eventually, well into the future, all communities collaborating to a high degree as a collective conscious caring society will feel as if they are one community worldwide. We know this is truly possible as we collaborate together and realise that this is our true destiny.

CHAPTER 3

GOVERNMENTS

The governments in our world have a tremendous effect on our societies.

Complaints from the public create more incentive and cooperation to get things right and to ensure there is democracy, with more human rights incorporated into the laws that we obey and live by, which invites a better standard for a peaceful world.

Governments will be more spiritually involved in the future. There will be a different relationship between governments and their citizens. Communication will take place between governments and the spirit world, which will be beneficial contact.

When proof of the afterlife is found, some people will be switched off to it, and therefore they will have trouble connecting to it and moving to a higher standard or high ground. Those in opposition or who cannot understand it will be left behind but will begin in time to understand and be beckoned toward it, and even they will adjust to it.

I myself am on high ground and am longing for, and open to help create, world peace.

The more pressure for human rights there is on governments, the more we can change what happens, so that what we want is incorporated. Protesting and agitating for rights creates controversy, which governments have to take into account, as it puts pressure on them to change their policies. It creates boundaries between protesters and governments, and the government rethinks things as it is hard to know what decisions to make. Progress can be slow: bit by bit. After the protests there are forums or gatherings which produce agreements between governments and citizens for human rights that they can be proud of. This is democracy at work.

Humans are outraged that wars are continuing in some countries, and they want to air their outrage.

Governments must think of ways to handle the plan for everyone to receive a fair share of care. Each citizen of every country will be cared for, and they will all know to share to have equality, so that everyone has human rights. It is important that the 'care and share' policy to bring equality is well done and agreed to. It takes time for people to adjust and agree, but it all goes along smoothly eventually.

At present the fact is that it is the darkest hour before the dawn (a new age term), meaning that people are horrified about the world situation and feel we are experiencing the worst-case scenario.

Because of people's resistance, even if they agree on something, those agreements do not always produce positive results straight away because of the time it takes to adjust. We are at a crossroads, because of wars, as we are in the fourth-dimensional transition, which is turbulent and causes confusion. Things have to get worse before getting better, as things have to get really bad before people demand change. I want to make it clear that world peace is possible.

Some people are trying to do good and want to come together for world peace, but it seems like they are in small numbers and small groups. But when we understand about the universe and the afterlife, there will be a concentrated effort to get things right and into the order of oneness for world peace.

We will be thankful for the proof of the universe's support; proof that there is an afterlife. This will allow us to think in different ways to what we do now, as we aim for the ideal world that we all desire. The exceptional proof that we will have of the afterlife and the universe is informative to those members of the public who have been denying it and not allowing it into their awareness. Proof from spirits in heaven will be okay with governments, and the spirits will make sure the proof is made known, and they will keep everything under control. Spirits are watching Earth all the time and working with governments energetically to keep things under control for human beings. Governments and spirits in heaven will come together with compatibility, and the governments will agree with what the spirits want.

All through time people have desired to have good lives, and to be informed and be compatible with others. The force of the spirit world will create strong energy for people to follow and progress.

Those who attain equality learn to share with others who are not so well off, and resources will be sent out so that everyone gets a fair share. All of my envisaging has brought to you a vision of the future you can trust.

Authorities will inform the public about a new beginning of achievement, from the orders put together by government, the leaders, and spirit, and this will convince you that you are capable of doing what you are given to do. Firm and progressive collaboration between governments and the public will work well to deal with the collective way of behaving. Our thoughts create our imagination to obtain our wishes, meaning that our mind creates our reality. What is in our imagination is what goes out into our real-life reality and creates what happens in our life, because our thoughts are very powerful in achieving what we want.

When we are in alignment with the new age, we will think it is funny (in a humorous way) how we used to treat people so badly and have wars in the third and fourth dimensions. It will be an honour to get everything right in a professional way for fifth-dimensional reality. Unifying the predominant mainstream current reality with fifth-dimensional reality will cause humour, as we will be happy with better behaviour, and we will have such a right mindset that it actually will seem funny, because we are transforming from the fourth dimension into the fifth dimension. We will all know what we are doing, and our professionalism will mean that the absolute best quality work will be done and done exactly right.

The beginning of the changes will be muddled with many different ideas suggested. The government has to untangle the muddle to get things right and to make the best decision for democracy, while also refining agreements and satisfying the spirit world's wishes. All citizens will have a voice and input into what is in the agreements, and they will persuade the government to do what they think is right that will ensure peace.

The more countries that either are, or become, democratic, and the more human rights they incorporate in their democracy, the more other countries will follow their example and also include human rights in their laws. The collaboration with teamwork really comes together with everyone working for what is best, to meet the demand for governments and citizens to get into the new frequency of the fifth dimension.

We will come together knowing the proof that the higher energy is connected rather than separate. There is knowing now that there is a higher energy there, rather than just believing it. The universe's power in action is shown when there is a thunderstorm, when the sounds and rainwater send a message of the force of the universe. After a storm or rain, often a rainbow will appear in the sky, and this is a sign of a bridge of connection with the universe.

Dictatorship

Let us take a look at the dictatorships in the world now, separately from democracies. All dictators have an extraordinary amount of power, and there is nothing that the citizens of those countries can do about it, and they know it. They use their tremendous power to support other dictators in the world with money and methods of enforcing their control. Anyone trying to speak out against, or oppose, the dictator in any way is imprisoned or executed, which is very manipulative and gives dictators total control and power to do whatever they want. They are hated by many people in their country and also in other countries, and if enough strong feeling builds up against them, they can get thrown out of power or assassinated. This can work out for the better if the dictator was horrendously terrible. The disastrous things inflicted by dictators, because of the amount of power they have, combined with the companionship they have with other dictators and their support of each other's power, gives them an even higher degree of power and control in their positions.

There are problems in the world caused by the many continuing wars, which concerns many democratic people, but dictators could not care less about the whole of the Earth and all the people on it. They only think about themselves, and because of their terrible attitudes, they just want to enrich themselves and keep their power, as this is the nature of dictatorships.

The leader, who is the dictator, and his inner circle of government officials around him who have the same attitudes as their leader, control everything and ignore anything they do not want to hear, and they make the citizens suffer. To keep their power, they imprison those who criticise them or are opposed to them, and their brutal police enforce their control. The public are encouraged to inform on each other, which creates fear in society and mistrust of the people in their life. If you say a word against the dictatorship to anyone you know, they could report you to the police/authorities, who may visit your home during the night and take you away, and you will not be seen again. Dictatorships commonly punish those who are against them. The huge level of hatred towards the dictator can eventually cause uprisings by armed rebels who fight the dictator's army, and this can be a long, drawn-out process.

Once all dictators are deposed and we have the one world democracy in the future, then all people in the world will want to work together in forgiveness, supported on by highly evolved citizens, especially as there will be cures for mental diseases. Until there is forgiveness, there will always be war and conflict, arguing and revenge that does not get resolved. Dictators are a symptom of the separation of humans, as they see their citizens as being separate from themselves, and so they do not allow human rights in their country.

Human rights need to be incorporated into the laws of countries. Until the dictators can be ousted, so that their greed and power and abuses are ended, a true democracy cannot be introduced.

Greed is a negative quality in any government, but it is possible to remove greedy politicians and authorities from power with strong universal support and all citizens uniting to make it happen.

Democracy

All the light people in the world, including myself writing this book, will embrace democracy worldwide, and as we understand the 'one' connection, we will all have forgiveness, which will help relieve tension.

We are at the crossroads of this transition/changeover time, and all the old garbage must be thrown out to get it out of the way, to bring in the new with the force of alignment with fifth-dimensional energy. All the new that comes in pushes out the old and lifts up the energy so things can work out better. The higher the lift in human consciousness, the quicker we will move into fifth-dimensional reality.

We must reframe our negative viewpoints, as it will not be necessary for humans to be negative anymore, so we will move on and learn positivity to have a new outcome.

Once we are in our evolved revolution in the future, we will have computer programmed robots to do tasks to help us out. Robots will be programmed to help us keep peace. They will be used by governments, and they will eventually be programmed with human feelings so they can work with us better and understand us better. Robots will eventually control us, and they will tell us what to do. This is good, as they will show us the right way to achieve peace, and they will make humans more civilised with better living standards that support wellbeing.

Peaceful ways will be put into law so that the way of living will lead to a peaceful world. Governments will analyse and discuss options to make the best laws for this purpose, so that all government corporations are aligned. Putting this into law results in a better life that is fun and enjoyable, and we enjoy working together to get peace. This is excellent for human rights and progress, and having robots in control will cause a huge leap forward for humans at a much faster rate, to live in an era of world peace.

Eventually, well into the future, when there does not have to be any governments, there will be no democracy either, as everyone will behave with human consideration and treat one another with caring and sharing. A lot has to happen before then!

All of the bad people from the old third dimension and fourth dimension that have done bad things will have their mental illnesses and diseases cured, and they will be able to move on with self-forgiveness, and to have self-worth with positive outcomes in their lives, which is a wonderful scenario.

It is exciting and invigorating during the transition time, to make the changes that have to be made in the in-between stage, as people want the fifth dimension and are looking forward to it. Each step in the sequence during the transition brings the fifth dimension a bit closer. Each part of each action that we take draws the fifth dimension nearer, as the changes are talked through, walked through and worked through. The actions rely on the alliance of the participants, and the implementing of the action relies on support as it travels through the change process. The walking through involves ironing out disagreements and issues between those taking part. Many issues are full of conflict and take such a long time to be resolved that people get tired of it and just want to give up. The issues that are so ingrained and stuck are best just being discarded.

In a strong democracy the cooperation of all people is encouraged, with all being treated equally, and it is hoped they will work together companionably, firstly for inner peace within themselves, and secondly, on a much larger scale, for a peaceful world.

As a generation of the population goes by there are a lot of changes in the government, which can be for the better, but there is always both good and bad that happens, and what is needed is to keep things balanced, steady and centered, without extremes. It is just a natural part of life on Earth, that no matter what happens, whether it is good or bad, it always has to work out for the better and be stable and balanced.

A balance of agreements that we can all understand, with cooperation, communication and coming together, need to be coordinated to convert to the fifth dimension, to move forward. There is a wealthy place of wellbeing that is within all of us, that is strong and golden inside us and makes us all fortunate to be able to move forward together into fifth-dimensional reality.

New age beliefs will become more ingrained in people as the ongoing wars in the fourth dimension, and the destruction they cause, unites people who fear that doomsday is about to arrive, and so they start to get their act together. There will be an outcry by citizens protesting to get rid of wars, to get the old ways out, and to have a new world, and although in dictatorships there cannot be protests, in democracies people will be demanding 'out with war' and 'in with peace'.

What a deliverance it is to the world when the population starts feeling the truth and begins working together cooperatively. The feeling of cooperation is so exhilarating that it spurs people on and inspires them to put aside their differences and focus on their common goal.

Humans realise that they can cooperate, but they do not realise it is what they HAVE to do for world peace, to keep out of a world of ongoing conflict and fear. When things are so bad in the world, you realise that cooperating reduces and then dissolves fear, as the teamwork creates a lot of companionship as well as an exceptional amount of love that is so important. The uplifting effect of companionship is flowing and sweeping events forward in a flourishing display like never seen before, like racing along a stream. When communities come together and thrive and flourish, they become like one big happy family.

Our wishes that are put out with our imagination progress into real life reality because we keep our focus on that. Now that we are in the fourth dimension at the crossroads, we are entitled to gather together to socially interact and work together in our communities with the government, towards a wonderful new reality. In the fourth dimension we have to put aside our differences that were dividing us and dividing the world. Individuals were not interacting as they felt entitled to have their different points of view.

A legal procedure is needed that will be enforced in the community by the citizens in order to move on and let go of the past.

Every spoken word and action have a strong effect and power, as the universe returns to us 100% of what we put out, and we have a full connection with everything, with no doubts, and we have automatic thankfulness. There are no doubts about the knowledge as it is truthful and convincing.

Democracy is vital as it is the best and most equitable system for human beings and communities, whereby governments and citizens put strong strategies in place to protect citizens rights and safety. Democracy has given women more say in their own lives and in society. New Zealand was the first country in the world to give women the right to vote. I think that is worth repeating since I am a New Zealander myself: New Zealand was first in the world, in 1893, to pass a law so that women could vote.

I feel enormous excitement inside my being to be a New Zealander. For men and women to both have an equal say in who their elected representatives would be, through voting, enhanced the possibility and hope of women in other countries for the same thing to happen there. Being born in New Zealand makes it feel meaningful to me that New Zealand has been a leader in women's rights in the world. This means a great deal to me as I have a strong sense of fairness and equality for everyone, and this means keeping everything in the government balanced, to do with the economy, fairness and sharing.

A Government Worldwide

As an increasing number of countries become democracies, human beings will gain the things they are entitled to. The more that things keep getting better and the more we all cooperate, then the easier and happier life will be for us. Democracies that keep getting stronger, and with humans having and using more intuition, empowers citizens to make powerful plans to get things right and to take a clear firm stance on what is right and wrong. The empowerment is stronger in countries that are the most peaceful, and are free of war and conflict, and which have a strong desire to do what is best for their citizens. This motivates all the other democracies to do the same.

Dictators can feel overpowered when a lot of their citizens want them out of power, and this can make them fearful, to the extent that they may run away to another country to avoid being assassinated. Their oppressed population get so tired of the dictator that they unite in a large group and form a revolution to overthrow him, so that they can have the chance to become a democracy and change the destiny of their country.

Powerful governments like America can often help other countries who have conflicts and wars by arranging peace talks and ceasefires. When all countries come together worldwide, they can give each other support and feel unified in their course of action, as they agree on the essential strategy and how to implement it. Alliances can be formed between nations collaborating to realign the smooth running of peace throughout the world, and to take the steps they need to take to ensure this smooth-running procedure.

A mindset is needed amongst all citizens and governments to unify, to get the biggest output with the best results possible for world peace. The intensity of focus propels things to move along faster, with the universe supporting us as we work with it, so that our good results are beyond what our imagination thought possible. This procedure has a uniting effect, and it is interesting and fun to make it happen.

Many people find it hard to believe that worldwide democracy is possible or will ever happen, but as time has gone by more countries have become democratic, as they oust dictatorships, and those citizens who support authoritarianism become outnumbered by democratic fighters and activists.

People want their day-to-day lives, where they are following the flow, to be lived in democratic conditions with human rights incorporated into law. At times they need to stop and evaluate the progress to ensure that they are going in the right direction. Sometimes there are a lot of conflicts and fights between different governments, or even with one government where there are different political parties, and also personality clashes that must be worked out, to have a peaceful democracy.

A worldwide democracy can only come to fruition if citizens feel safe and comfortable and have inner peace within themselves, which they have to have for worldwide peace to happen.

Dramatic changes are taking place in so many countries that we can clearly see the 'darkest hour before the dawn' is happening in these places.

I expect China to be the new superpower in the future. Their huge manufacturing output in recent decades has made China noticeably richer, and they export their goods to a lot of other countries, which is a major achievement. In time to come, China will change so dramatically that it seems likely that it will be in control as the world's most powerful country. The one worldwide government is likely to be located there, and this will be accepted by the world's population, as all governments will relocate there as one unified government.

The growth of spiritual development can happen very quickly. Governments will know the spirit world and will command that spirituality is incorporated in laws. We know that spirituality is there because we feel the frequency of the new energy, although we may not realise that a new world is going to arrive, because of the wars and confusion.

One worldwide government that is acknowledged by all citizens who are much more spiritually informed, can happen very quickly and dramatically, spontaneously and enthusiastically!

CHAPTER 4

WORLD ECONOMY

Imbalances in the economy have always disrupted the lives of many people, and crime has always been a problem.

We are waking up by developing more code systems and putting them into use, making them strong and secure so that the coding systems cannot be breached and the pin numbers cannot be guessed.

Ongoing failures of systems have not worked out for customers internationally. A whole new level of thinking is required to lead the change for the economy and lift the democratic system to a whole new level, to replace the paper money (cash) system, and to inspire a dream or vision of world peace. The code system is non-violent and has no crime.

The advantage of the code system is to have one worldwide, standard, secure system. This will bring the world together in their commitment to a fifth-dimensional coding system that changes society. Co-operation between all countries to develop a high-quality system will bring profound stability to the world economy. The strength of the system will stop dishonesty, theft, crime, misuse, unfairness and inequality. The new incoming generation will find every aspect of their lives is better and will appreciate the reliable, trustworthy system in the new world that they will live in.

The process of developing the new coding system must be well thought-out and well planned. Major refurbishing needs to be done to balance out the fluctuations in the economy. The procedure of transitioning from the paper money (cash) to the code system will happen easily and quickly because all world leaders will want to contribute to it. A domino effect will happen as more and more leaders of countries agree to it, and the process can be done easily by automatic means.

World leaders and citizens who cannot adjust to the new coding system will get left out at first, but eventually they will understand that they have to follow what everyone else is doing. The circumstances of people's lives; their work, leisure, education, etc., will be interpreted and put into the coding system. Every aspect of their lives will be incorporated into the coding system. This coding system is for the benefit and good of all people. It will keep people honest; they won't be able to steal the information.

There is an electromagnetic field that is computerised into every person on Earth when they become part of the coding system. Inside the palm of your hand will be a magnetic form of computerised information, so that people will simply need to scan their hand over a scanning machine when they buy things, and for identification when necessary. Although the coding system will be controlling, people will understand the advantages of it, and they will see how it keeps things balanced in society and know how useful it is.

The coding system will help to bring people together and help lead people to world peace.

When people see that the coding system is having a domino effect to help people, then they will be more committed to following the process needed for them to have the coding implanted in them.

Knowing how to process and balance the world economy automatically to create world peace, and the commitment to achieving world peace, is the leading aim, with the support of all people. The economy will speak for itself as it is no longer in crisis.

The coding system will be very powerful, and it will bring us all together.

There will be no crime, as nothing but the truth will spill out from the worldwide code system, which cannot be tampered with in any way by criminals. The wonderful achievement of the coding system will be to manifest a non-violent, peaceful world. Money is a huge incentive for criminals to be violent and dishonest, and once they can no longer obtain money unlawfully and by violent means, this removes a lot of violence in society caused by money.

Energetic encounters, which happen when people buy things, are tripling. People are developing more acceptance of the coding system idea. This fits in with the domino effect; when some people begin to accept the idea of the coding system, the idea snowballs, and this leads to more and more people having acceptance. Those people who are against the idea will, in maybe a year or two, gradually fall into place with the others who have already accepted it. The numbers of people that will support the coding system will guarantee its success.

An equal income for all people will be guaranteed, no matter what work they do, or even if they are not working or not able to work. Everyone will get the same income, and no one will have to struggle to have enough to live on. Everyone's financial situation will have balance, and they will be able to pay their bills.

By using numbers in the coding system, this prevents any misinformation. The outcome and result of the worldwide coding system will be extreme fairness and accuracy for world peace. Governments will approve the coding system to be used. Then people with technological expertise will put it into action. It will all flow into place. It will follow on from the coding system already in use in society, whereby we use plastic cards with pin numbers. Then people, once they have received the coding system for themselves, will figure out the best way to use it for themselves and work to make it happen and to get the coding system into place.

Everything is connected; all people, as well as the universe, and as people work together, the universe works to support us. The world cannot carry on with hatred. We have to consider changing everything in time, before there is complete disaster in society caused by fear and accompanying violence. Thinking about balancing the economy makes the code system the way to go.

We need a code system that performs very well and suits the needs of the people. Understanding the code system will lead to its success! The quality and benefits of this system will be spread through society by word of mouth, making a stronger domino effect. Using the coding system will lead to the wellbeing of the people. Then the ongoing process of using the coding system will gather everything together that is necessary for world peace to come about. This will complete the implementation of the coding system.

Starting up the new coding system is the hardest part, as it is a completely new thing for people to get used to. The transition to the new system is a huge change for people, and many people do not like change. They are set in their normal routines and ways of doing things. Even though they are told how good the change will be, it is still hard for them as it disrupts their current habits. However, the introduction of the new system will take priority over people's reluctance to change.

Every part of people's lives will be affected. All work will be paid the same amount. All jobs will be seen as equally good, just different. The coding system will have to be worked out to suit all circumstances of all people. The technology experts will have to figure out how to do this. They will make the system fair for everyone.

When someone buys something, there is a connection made between the buyer, the coding system and the seller. It shows all the information, and the identities of those involved are also recorded by the technology centre. The technical programming makes the system powerful because of the safety, security and extreme fairness. People will like the system and feel good about it, and it will have a unifying effect worldwide. They will go about their daily lives with a feeling of wellbeing. They will feel free because of the safety of the system that has been put in place.

Equal prosperity for everyone, along with fairness and kindness, enables widespread peace in the world that continues.

When travellers and tourists go to other countries it will be much easier when the coding system is in use. It will standardise and unify the travel experience throughout the world. Entering and leaving other countries, and travelling within them, will be the same easy and safe procedure regarding identification and paying for things, with people scanning the palms of their hands on scanning machines. It will be the same unified system in all countries so that the different money currencies in different countries will not matter. Travellers will not exchange their own currency for that of the country they are going to; it will not be necessary.

What a powerfully better system this one-world coding system will be, with the alignment of the people and the system. Inside the coding system, all data on each person is stored. When a person scans the palm of their hand, their details show up. Their name, address, income and banking all come up on screen on the machine. Customers will understand the system and how it works and will see on the screen the amount of the purchase taken off their bank balance. It will be obviously clear to people when they see what happens, and they will have full agreement about what is done.

Theft of someone's cash, bank cards and identity cards by a criminal holding a knife or a gun, and threatening harm, will no longer happen. People will lose their fear of theft. Computer hacking of bank accounts will not be possible, as bank accounts will be in the coding system and will be ingrained in your hand. The exceptional security keeps the worldwide economy safe.

We are now in the fourth dimension, which is the changeover between the material world and the spiritual world. Everything is changing: the economy, education, race and culture, family and community, spirituality (which is becoming more accepted), and homosexuality (which is more accepted). There will be an ending to poverty, pollution and diseases, nationalism and xenophobia, and war will transform into peace through justice. Time is increasing in pace. When we were still in the third dimension (up until the early 2020s), everything was slow and held people back in all areas of life (as listed above). By entering the fifth dimension, in 2032/2033, an alignment between the material world and the spiritual world will happen; that will be the Age of Aquarius.

The powerful coding system will be so strong, fair and appropriate that it will control and stop anyone who would want to spread lies and misinformation. Also, the system will not be expensive to set up and put into use and will be economical to operate because of its structure. For a brighter future, we need the knowledge now of how to refurbish the economy. By moving forward with putting the new coding system into use, along with that will come the safety and reliability of the numbers that the system runs on and the pin number of each person.

Courtesy, politeness and consideration towards people go alongside the running of the system. There will be many, many coding technicians in local communities to teach people about the new system, and how to use it, as they will implant the coding system into people's hands.

There will be one worldwide government. There will be a coalition of all the governments of the world's countries coming together as one. Eventually, the worldwide economy will be so efficient that government will not be needed. The coding system will be the economy and will be like a government, as it will hold all the information.

Technology will be developed in such clever ways that a computer will be worn like a wristwatch. This computer watch will be aligned with the encoded palm of the hand, and with the blood system of the wearer. It will be such powerful technology that it will be able to tell the human what food and how much food is best for them to buy, as well as what clothes and how many clothes.

Our human brains will have a computerised connection with an electromagnetic field by wearing a band on our heads, like a headband. This will give us magnified memories. It will connect with our brain cells, so that they grow and connect for their full potential. This band will only need to be worn for a certain length of time, until the brain is

100% connected. A signal, or beeper, will sound when 100% is reached. It would be too overpowering to wear the band for longer, after it is at 100% connection. People will see how good it is, and therefore it will become compulsory before long.

With everything put into place with a computerised coding system (palm, wrist, and head devices), the electromagnetic effect will ease pressure in our daily lives. We will be aligned with the economy. We will be aligned with our mind and grounded with our body. We will be centered with our spirit as we come into the fifth dimension.

CHAPTER 5

A NEW EDUCATION

I will describe what I mean by a new education and what it will be like.

Children have to go to school each day, learning things they do not enjoy, and being bullied by other children. They take risks by wagging school because they are scared of the bullies and cannot confront them because the bullies have stronger power. Bullies are unhappy within themselves, and that is why they take out their feelings on other people to hurt them.

This book is a meeting place for those who aspire to change the education system. Those who want progress that is right for their children, and who have the belief and understanding and knowledge to ignite complete change, can unite to determine the right way to go. A good proportion of people will want substantial change. A considerable amount of effort by mature adults will be needed, and it will be a gradual process over time, involving upheaval, transformation and cooperation.

The curriculum will be changed, and also the way children are taught. Learning will be fun and enjoyable as there will be a whole new way of learning. All subjects will be combined into one subject as 'Oneness Education.' Classrooms will be of better quality and in better condition with heating and air-conditioning. Teachers, parents and children will cooperate to get things right. This will be new age education, and those who initiate the movement for change will inspire others to follow on and continue it. The education system will thereby be naturally lifted into the fifth dimension.

All the old data used to educate children now, in the third dimension, will be manoeuvred out of use, so that a cycle of new learning skills can be established. Here is the new age coming in bringing progress; this is a fact, as the old structure of the education system is phased out.

Adjustment to the new incoming education will be accomplished through the support and cooperation of all those involved, as they all work together with the aim of moving education ahead. As people become more aware of the failings of the current education system, and that their children are not interested in learning what is currently available, they are changing their thoughts. This leads the way to the fifth dimension.

A common perception is that the set ways of the current education system are too difficult to change. This has resulted in postponing possible changes that do not fit into the ordinary system, as people think it is too hard to live out their dreams of teaching children in a way that improves the world. They feel the dream is too big to achieve, and they doubt that the future that they imagine will ever be possible, no matter how much they dream. Things would change faster and much further if these people were able to shift their beliefs.

When they realise that they can shift their belief from thinking it is too difficult, to thinking it is possible, they will feel much better.

Progress can then be made that leads to success and benefits for their children.

Delivering a new education system is the right thing to do. It will spark the children's prospects and chances to live successfully in the new age. Children will feel privileged to attend school as it will be to their advantage and in their favour.

The knowledge that is coming in for the new age must be integrated by the government's Department of Education. This knowledge will seem extraordinary to people, and they will need to come to grips with it. Extreme coordination will be done to bring all the new knowledge together for teachers and children, and this must be done in a considerate, well-mannered way. This knowledge is all around us and is eternal but is not known about because to access the knowledge, we need to be aligned with fifth-dimensional reality. Instead of merely checking out the knowledge and passing on by, we must give it the importance it deserves and come together with the common goal of using and integrating it.

Our wellbeing will be transformed by the reprogramming and transformation of our ideas and concepts. We are very capable of transforming when we know the wellbeing we will have. Eternal concepts that require deep thought, and that come from powerful universal knowledge, will overtake current undermining ideas.

Universal knowledge transforms according to each person's capability to understand it, and how important it is for them to have that knowledge. Over time, they may increase their level of knowledge as their level of understanding rises.

Knowledge from the fifth dimension will be gathered into a new database. Profound new understanding will show us that we have to be better people and that we will gain by living life to the full.

Everything ingrained in us in the past, that we assumed was true, must be seen in the light of the new understanding. In retrospect, our past understanding was true for that time.

Agreements will be composed in the government's Department of Education so that all teachers will know what to teach in the fifth-dimensional reality.

In a conduction process, old ways will be thrown out, to bring in and establish the new cosmic era known as the Age of Aquarius. This will be exciting.

By reading this book, you will know the factual truth about fifth-dimensional reality in the context of letting go, accepting new beliefs, and feeling the excitement and privilege of learning. Our mind has enormous capacity for learning. In its deep subconscious, our mind can have a whole new belief, which creates a new human reality. The outstanding significance of this is that the knowledge that is needed to live in a far better world is already inside us, as well as the way we interpret it in the new age that is coming in. An attitude change is needed to get the new outcome. Behind every idea and attitude must be love.

The action of humans all working together purifies negativity, so we can live in a whole new world where there is understanding and agreement that we are all one and live as all one. Oneness education is opening up an understanding in us that we are not separate from each other, that we are all connected as one. We will come together in the new era of love, to live a better life.

Everyone, as a collective, will work together to make things better. Doing the work progresses stability on Earth, so that achievements can be made, and the work will bind with our essence, which is the basis of who we are. Universal energy supports us automatically when we all work together.

Excitement will build among people, who will be intrigued by the new knowledge. This will accelerate the momentum, which needs to happen to access more and more knowledge, so that the stream of new information will become a wonderful flood.

Everyone will know what they have to do and will feel positive about what is happening. It is an important central point that everyone on Earth will be coming together and working together, and the universe then supports our thoughts and the wellbeing of our physical bodies and supports the emotional healing of people as well as the healing of the planet and its environment.

The new knowledge inspires more and more achievements to take place in the atmosphere of oneness.

There is a positive effect created by the position of the other planets in our solar system to bring in a new energy frequency, awareness and order for the new cosmic era.

There is going to be a lot of opposition from authorities fighting back against the new attitudes and changes. This will cause confusion in people as they will not know what to do. Corruption in governments and authorities can make things tricky, and this will be ongoing for some time, until people receive the knowledge for the new fifth-dimensional age.

By knowing what is right in fifth-dimensional reality, you are in the best place to see straight away what you want to receive.

You are meant to be reading this book. I have experienced 'Journey' work with professional practitioners, and I have understood the joy that has brought me to this work. Because of my essence, I am writing this book to inspire others.

Oneness education is all about learning what is right and wrong. We will all have a clear, exact sense of right and wrong with everything we do. Wrongs done in the past in the third-dimensional reality will not happen again, as we will know better.

We have the ability within each one of us to progress. If we align ourselves with our own ability we can communicate better about what is right, to resolve things in the world to have world peace.

To communicate better, you need to know what is better for you, especially with the physical body, by being grounded, centered and aligned within yourself. By meditating or doing positive affirmations, you can be more connected to yourself and what is best for you. Clear your mind, be more spiritual, and wake up to a whole new world of enjoyment.

Over time, the education curriculum has been improved, reviewed and discussed, but it has to be totally changed. People are pushing for more democracy and for more human rights, and this has been an ongoing process for a long time. There is pressure to give people more rights, and for this to happen people must use their own intuition to know where to go and what to do to be effective in obtaining rights.

Some people protest in the streets in an organised peaceful protest, others may write to their elected officials, their local representative in government, or to the leaders of their country. Others may form groups with like-minded people who have the same ideas and are fighting for the same rights. Groups can have more power in society and be listened to and noticed more, because of the power gained from their larger numbers.

Agitating for change will bring results. Going through the transitional changeover time of the fourth dimension will be a confusing time. But keeping on pushing forward with protests and unrest and a lot of debate will cause things to slowly begin to change. This slow start will increase in speed, and those opposed to change will change their stance and make agreements to work together with positivity and understanding.

There is a duty to teach the new data because it is right, and it is positive.

Even if progress takes a long time, it is vitally important to learn about what will be needed in the fifth dimension. We need to know more about the universe and what everything is all about, and we need to learn about our connection to everything in the universe. New education also teaches us how to relate to each other and how to interact with each other.

The universe will wrap you in its powerful warmth to enable you to do what you are supposed to do. Everything is coordinated, in place and ongoing; that is the action of the universe.

To maintain wellbeing, we must be flexible. Moving from the third dimension to the fifth dimension is a big leap. Transitioning through the fourth dimension involves a lot of crises and upsetting things happening in the world. Being flexible will get us through the fourth dimension and into the fifth.

The momentum of the power of the universe and its teaching, and the alignment of the planets, gives us power and supports us, and leads to ongoing success.

When we all work together, it programs the universe to help us.

People must become aware of the bad things in the world and connect with others who are also aware, in order to stop the harmful people. Enough good people can undo the bad. When people do not know what to do and they stand confused, it is challenging to confront the bad. They must speak up and say what they know is right. People support democracy to the best of their ability with the education they have.

The true value of oneness education is that people enjoy socialising and interacting on a much higher level of oneness.

Children in classrooms will be socially interacting while enjoying learning; this is the best of oneness education. No one will be harmed or left out, as the attitude is that all children progress well together, and are self-reliant.

I cannot emphasise enough that education must be stress-free with no fuss or worry, and that all those involved; the Department of Education, teachers, parents and children, must all share the same goals and vision and be supportive of each other.

To bring change requires large numbers of people wanting changes and agitating for change and also involves a lot of communication and social support.

Everyone must receive a fair deal from the education system. This requires a large amount of cooperation to ensure the new system is fair to everyone and gives all students an equal fair benefit. Releasing all the old ways of education will open the way for a new education that serves the students rightfully with equal advantages for their good.

Equality of education will result in a population that is equally educated, so that people will be able to identify with each other and feel equal, giving them a feeling of belonging and oneness with others. It will deliver the identity to children that they deserve, so that they feel part of the oneness of all humans and feel they are a valuable part of the population. Although they still have their individuality, they feel a sense of unity, equality and like-minded peaceful living with others. This gives them a feeling of profound meaningfulness, that makes them brighter and happier, as they see the common-sense prevailing around them in the world.

Fortunately for future schoolchildren, the great change in

education will be strongly focused on the new enlightened curriculum on a worldwide basis, setting the scene for world peace. Educators will have realised the need to focus on a way of teaching that will actually support peace in society, and the importance of applying their teachings to everyday living.

It seems like we are not getting anywhere in the world at the moment, with all the confusion. We feel as if we are on a roundabout that does not stop, and we cannot get off. Things appear to be getting worse in the world, with wars, conflicts, natural disasters and negativity. But things will get worse before they get better. Once this negativity is ended and we move into the fifth dimension, we will know where we are going.

Belief in a new education system, and the belief that transformation will happen, brings it into real life reality. This is new age theory, that strong belief as well as the action taken to speak up, and push for change, results in the attainment of what you want.

Transformation of the current status quo in society will happen; it is a fact. Many types of action must be pursued. Deep insight is needed to see the truth of what needs to be done.

Future schoolchildren, in large numbers, are the ones who will demand peace, as they see clearly what is not working for peace in the current world. They see what is wrong and that huge changes are needed to create the world that they want to live in.

At the moment, we are still going through the 'darkest hour before the dawn' (a new age term), and we are living with confusion.

My vision is that we are heading toward a better world once the current confusion is over and we come out of the 'darkest hour'. The sunrise is within sight, but the confusion must first be ended so that the sun rises for world peace.

Communication is fast in today's world. Computers spread information instantaneously. Those who are interested in, or concerned about, education and want changes can easily keep up with what is happening throughout the world.

More people are naturally moving out of old age ways of thinking and finding out about the new age information, and they are developing new ways of thinking. They have been affected by their own experiences and are thinking for themselves as a result.

From my written work in this book, what may happen is that many people may agree with my words and follow these ideas.

The frequency of the energy is higher now we are in the transition. It is making people more aware and focused; they are changing their thoughts in a whole new way to a new order of thinking. From the 'Journey' work that I have done, I know that a lot of change can be made, and I know the importance that beliefs and strong desire for change can have. I want to write this book in a way that keeps people grounded, aligned and centered.

We will feel good and feel proud of ourselves when we have taken the action that is needed both within ourselves and out in the world. There is a new age saying that 'what you believe you will receive'. I say to you that what you perceive, you will believe and will receive. Perceiving is when we sense things by getting a feeling about them and notice and realise things for ourselves. We will receive when we believe what we are sensing and realising.

In our current world, people have deeply held beliefs about certain facts and about how things should be in society and in the world. But they are only the facts that they are able to see at present. Universal planetary alignments will support the softening of their strong beliefs in those facts, so people will realise that there are other ideas, other ways and other facts that they were not able to see or hear about before.

The 'Journey' work process is very familiar to me, and I always refer to it in everything, regarding my childhood upbringing, to maintain a healthy way of living, and how to adjust to the incoming changes.

The comparison between the old third-dimensional lifestyle, to new fifth-dimensional living, shows dramatic transformation that will last forever. I will keep living this for the rest of my life. I have been shown in my vision of the future, the promise that you will be better people with a better way of living, in a happier world.

Will the world have everlasting peace? There is no need to worry. The idea is that if the Earth is ever threatened, our space travel will be so advanced that we will be able to escape the Earth as a species and travel far away to another planet.

I know it is easy to say that if we have world peace then we will not have struggles and life lessons to learn from. Fortunately, we do keep learning in a peaceful world. There are always lessons of experiencing what peace is like. We also learn to share with each other and be caring and kind to others. This keeps strengthening our souls.

Our mission is to get world peace. Working together will achieve this. The domino effect of the good things (people and actions) completely does away with the bad.

We are coming up to a long period of peace that will last 2000 years, the length of time of the Age of Aquarius. The past 2000-year period was the Age of Pisces, with its wars and male dominance. Astrology charts of the universal process of planets will be studied.

Teachers will be highly trained, so they do their job well. It is a whole new way of being at school as the main focus is on enjoyment.

Teachers will teach about oneness and will care about all students in their class, and they will be well paid.

Students will respect the teaching ability of their teachers and there will be no control issues in the classrooms. New teaching coming in, with the new teaching abilities, will deliver the education that is the best for the students.

Oneness education is awesome!

It is eternal, as there is always more learning and achievement to be obtained.

CHAPTER 6

RELIGIONS TRANSFORM

It would be nice to see religious conflicts at an end, never to be seen again. Currently there are conflicts and fighting for control by religions wanting their side to win, to have revenge and power over the other side. The truth is that religions want power over people to control the way they think, to make them believe that the church is right and they deserve what the church is teaching. What people recognise about religion is that the systematic teaching they have had is wearing out for them over time, as they are thinking and interpreting for themselves. Religion will be downgraded because of all the conflict and weariness with religion in general, and it will eventually work its way out into one spiritual religion worldwide. There will be a lot of future vitality as we all move by working our way into one new type of religion. As we are already moving into spirituality, the changeover from religion will be an easier process. Old religious doctrines will be left behind, and we will take on new spiritual doctrines that are more open and allow for freedom of thought.

Society must do a good job of fighting to end religions. Those who are interested in the new spirituality will face pressure from religious leaders, family members or the church community to stay in the religion, but they must fight against this pressure and follow their leaning to spirituality. The churches have power and have control over their followers who must obey church rules and doctrine, or they are told they will go to the devil when they die and live in everlasting punishment. This control is so forceful, with the use of fear, that it causes churchgoers to agonise over what to do and how to confront these issues. Some church members can stand up for themselves, and they leave their church to go in another direction with others who have a more enlightened way of living, with the new age.

The power of the universal energy in the new era is calling people toward it. Members of society hear this call and leave the old to follow the new, due to their ways of thinking and the teachings from the new. Some find it easy to transcend religion, whilst others find it difficult as their beliefs are very ingrained. There is always a way, though, to move away and out of religion.

Humans see all the conflicts occurring in the world and agree that religion is the biggest cause of them. Religious believers may think that by having conflicts with other religions or branches of their own religion, it will kill them off, and then believers will all join their religion, which they think is the only 'right' religion. It is no wonder there is so much confusion caused by religious beliefs; each religion, or sub-group or denomination of a religion thinks they are right. It is crazy, but also ridiculous that they have so much power, and the worst churches use it in bad ways by threatening their followers with harm if they leave their religion. Others may be shunned or be shown disapproval in their communities. Often their social life and friendships revolve around the church, making it hard to leave behind.

Church leaders want to keep their power and their rituals, and the belief system that goes with it, with their god(s) and a messiah.

The way to go is to call out for help about what to do and how to get through the upheaval of changing over and coming together as we wish to.

Special programs will turn beliefs around by comparing the religious and spiritual beliefs so that religious beliefs can be transferred over to spiritual ones. By making it clear how the two beliefs would go together, and then seeing them separately, by teaching them both and clarifying them, and by learning what is right and wrong with them both, makes everything right for transferring religious beliefs to spirituality. Religion needs to be seen in a new way, showing that its belief systems and dogmas are not true, to be able to solve conflicts.

Oneness education will help with the connection, where religions become more involved with spirituality, and the upheaval of religious transformation takes place. It just automatically happens by itself of its own accord that religion fades out more and more, leading to transformation. The contraction of religion, and the expansion of spirituality, will lead to the fulfilling of the destiny of a spiritual brotherhood. We will move away from churches and religions; they are not going to last and will empty out, and a spiritual brotherhood will eventuate. Coming out of religion is beneficial to spirituality and is supportive to the lives of those people. It will seem fair to those who have gone through the upheaval and have had the bravery to leave.

Since the mid twentieth century, the ingrained religions and set beliefs have gradually decreased due to transitions over time to a new era, and new enlightenment, with people more aware of themselves and having their own way of thinking.

The abandoning of religion opens the way for us to move forward with spiritual practices to be held in churches, halls and rooms. Out with the old and in with the new! This is a brave new beginning with the development of a unifying program. This unity does away with fear and defies religion, which fades out. New skills in action with spirituality, with all of us working together, are supported by the universal energy.

Information such as in these writings will remind those gathering together and working hard with each other how beneficial everything will be. We will compromise like never before in excitement to get things right. People will question religion after they leave, and the scriptures will have to be replaced. Beneficial statements will be made, with strategies from the new spiritual scriptures incorporated for people to live by, after the changes. When religion is transformed, new facts and data and questions about religion will form a spiritual reference book.

Scriptures and historical items dug up by archaeologists over time, and the facts and understanding that they learn about the past, makes sense of past history. Archaeologists put the pieces together like a puzzle, and match up the facts to make things more logical using their wisdom and knowledge.

People's perspectives will continue transitioning towards getting things right on a scale that adds up to alignment that is even and makes sense, to transcend the old scriptures and replace them with new ones incorporating the new knowledge that they understand. With the new scriptures being incorporated, it will end all religious conflict and bad behaviour in churches and religions.

You will receive 100% combined coordination when you move through the old religion towards the new, working your way out and developing, by applying what you have learned from your new skills and your new understanding of your intrinsic identity.

A lot of new age spirituality will be incorporated into school curriculums to have a new education about it at school. It will be a much easier understanding of spirituality with the oneness education in schools.

As all old scriptures move aside and new ones come in, everyone will realise that no religions are any good and it is best to do away with them and instead have a new perfect connection. The poor quality of their behaviour will fade away and then will begin the good behaviour of looking after each other. Religion is supposed to be loving, kind and generous to others. There is nothing wrong with religious followers having different beliefs from each other; it is the conflicts and killing that are bad and unacceptable, and this has been happening for untold centuries now. Religious believers think that their religion and beliefs are right, and the others are wrong, and they do not want anything to do with them. They think their god(s) would love them to kill off all others of other religions so that everyone will have a set belief under one religion - theirs!

There is no right or wrong in the mind game of life. Your reality is caused by what you think, as the energy of your thoughts returns to you 100%. There is no judgement of your thoughts; the universe cannot judge as it consists of everything that is, and it has no personality to make judgements with. It doesn't really matter what you think; it just comes back to you as you are producing energy from yourself with your thoughts. However, your thoughts do matter if you want good things to happen in your life. If you want world peace it is important to have good thoughts to produce positive outcomes, as the universe is so fully connected to us that it supplies right back to us the result of the energy of our thoughts. Even one single thought can have a big effect if you keep thinking that same thought over and over so that it produces an outcome equivalent to what you are putting out.

With religion there is an enormous cause and effect, because of bad conflicts and the punishment in the attitudes of church leaders.

As archaeologists find new scriptures and they are incorporated into a new book, this will have a large impact on religion to change. It will be true ancient wisdom that still applies today, but in a new way, rewritten for today's world and today's people. The new book will have a lot of meaning, whereas the religions will seem useless with no meaning for the new age, and they fizzle out completely as more spiritual things are introduced into the world. Then the concept of religion will no longer exist.

Religious conflicts are never enjoyable, and, along with the religious attitudes, judgmentalism, the fear of punishment by a god(s) and the lack of freedom of thought, does not give a good impression of religion. News coverage of religious conflicts puts the public off religion as they get tired of hearing about it and they see the negativity of it.

The greater your understanding of your thinking is, the more maturity you have to understand that your thinking creates the outcome in your own reality. You realise you must change your thoughts if you want a different outcome, and you are more aware of your thoughts and how to control them, to create the things you want in your life. Individual selves know that the support from others provides a connection to them that helps them to understand. It takes a while to connect in certain aspects as everyone sees it differently, but with the support of the universe it helps us to all think the same.

Because of the set beliefs in religion, it takes religious believers time to work their way out so that we can all be together and thinking the same. The churches have less power as time goes by as church members are integrating to a new alignment, with the universe's support and within themselves, as the universe is in a new alignment with the planets in our solar system.

The place called 'hell' only exists in people's minds; it is not an actual location. It may seem to people that it is a real place, as their mind creates their reality, and this makes it seem real.

However, churchgoers can still have a voice to be heard, as their strong belief and faith is what keeps them going and comforts them when they have hardships to endure throughout their lives.

There are some good churches that help the poor in their communities without requiring the recipients of their help to go to their church or adhere to their beliefs. They do it to be kind, helpful and fair to the disadvantaged and needy in their community, as they think this is the right thing for them to do. This sharing and giving to others less fortunate creates a more widespread, kinder and caring religious community.

Members of the church community can get the most out of their churchgoing by enjoying each church service, having a nice chat and cup of tea with other members afterwards, then by going home and discussing the service and the preaching with their family. After that, continue going to the service each week and see what you get out of it, and compare your own beliefs to the church's beliefs, and notice any differences.

Currently, some churches are taking a more lenient attitude towards the beliefs of their congregation and not forcing them to believe things that they do not want to. Because of this, churchgoers are becoming more familiar with their own mind and what they want to believe, being conversant with church beliefs and looking into spiritual beliefs. As the abandoning of religion increases, church leaders will give in to their followers and it will be easier for the churchgoers to consider different beliefs, which is fairer to them.

By putting all church beliefs together on one side, and all spiritual beliefs together on the other side, you can compare the differences and adjust how you are seeing each of them, from how each group are seeing it; the spiritual group and the religious group. Friction can result, from people having to adjust to other's beliefs, between churchgoers and everyone else (the non-believers), when people go their own way with their beliefs.

As time goes on spiritual beliefs will increase and become more accepted as religion becomes emptied out, leading to an evolved outcome where spiritual beliefs continue on without any contraction or anything in the way. A contraction would occur when something gets in the way of spiritual beliefs becoming accepted. This would need to be looked at to determine if the hindrance is a good thing or a bad thing that controls what we do, so that we cannot move forward to do what we want to do that is for our benefit.

Because we are heading into a much freer world with more personal power, and authorities do not have so much power over individuals, anything that is contracting is becoming a thing of the past. To deal with the contractions, release them, let them go. They will be eliminated by the evacuation of religion as it fades out, due to its old concepts that no longer work for people.

It is sometimes thoughtfully said that religion has good doctrine and strong beliefs that believers can have faith in to give them hope and endurance in their often-difficult lives. But religion is always fear-based, preaching about the devil and god's judgement, so that if you do not behave as the church says and follow the beliefs, you will not go to heaven. I have mentioned before that you need certain fears to protect you from danger, and similarly in religion, if you give your life to God, you will be protected from the devil. But this is also about the churches having too much power over their followers.

Once religion is transformed and eliminated to its core, giving way to the movement of what is found in spirituality, there will be no more of the fear that was in religion; it will not exist anymore. There is a lot of doubt in religion from non-believers, and also a lot of knowing from ingrained beliefs, and the further it evacuates out, the more things speak for themselves as people incorporate spirituality more. Just by continuing on with our daily lives and seeing the transformation unfolding, we will progress towards the unity we desire under one faith.

Fear of the devil is used by religion, which puts the dark side of negativity into their beliefs, making a devil spirit-being human-like, with the same emotions as humans. The male dominance of the Piscean age, with the control they had over others, created separateness with their power to have humans believe they are separate from everything else. This leads to confusion, therefore, because there is so much power to create war and conflicts. This should be eliminated; it belongs to the past, and churches know that their god(s) hates (giving 'him' a human emotion) revengeful fighting in the world. Conflicts cause confusion in believers; for instance, they think the devil they believe in is possessing people and making them commit bad deeds. God(s) would not want humans fighting and hurting each other, nor would the god(s) want to torment humans with everlasting damnation and throwing them into a lake of fire, as the churches teach. This is just to scare churchgoers and give them fear that they cannot reincarnate but will be trapped in 'hell' for eternity. The Christian Bible says that there is no reincarnation into another life after we die. Church believers do not listen when non-believers say there is no devil, as they think the non-believers do not know the 'truth' of the church teachings and need to be 'saved' to believe in God.

Fear of separateness can be overcome when we stick together and connect with our work. We will understand, as individuals, that in the new Age of Aquarius everything is connected and there will not be any understanding of separateness.

Everyone will understand the way to see Agnosticism, by finding proof of the afterlife/heaven and proof that all particles are connected with us, and that the whole universe is 100% connection, so there is nothing separate to research into. Nothing can be separate if everything is connected. God is not separate. The devil does not exist, but the bad deeds and evil in the world that churches attribute to the devil are done by humans from their minds and from human bad behaviour that comes from within them. Those humans were meant to do their deeds on Earth and that was obviously part of their essence being here in the Piscean age.

As we move into the Age of Aquarius, we realise that everything we do, every idea, and every outcome that happens is connected for our wellbeing. If the universal energy was separate from us there is no way we could be working together with its support to get things right in the world and to have that connection.

We have to know that we are all connected. To achieve what we want to find, we all have to work together to find world peace in our mind and everywhere else out around us. We will realise the goal can be achieved when everything is put into place and it flows as a whole, as everything is worked in together for the entire peace of us all.

CHAPTER 7

LADDERS INTO SPIRITUALITY

Ladders make you climb upwards; they have steps, and they resonate with moving up towards higher action that could be of some advantage. You are moving up higher to spirituality when you go up these steps. They are good for climbing, although there is still fear connected with ladders, because you know you can fall off the ladder or back down its steps, and possibly injure yourself by having a bad accident. However, they really are able to move us up to a higher state of consciousness, which means that this will be a very interesting chapter.

Many lightworkers are here working hard to heal the planet, using their spiritual traditions to awaken others. Ladders are associated with transcendence from this material world, and also transformation on the Earth plane. Lightworkers are occupied with the physical hard work of facilitating the changes to spirituality for world peace.

Some people here in the material world neglect spirituality because they have a negative attitude. If we want to be positive, we cannot focus on the bad things as it only drags us down. We can be positive and climb to the very top of the ladder to have a full understanding of spirituality. This is very exciting; it is enough to make everything spin clockwise at exceptional speed, that makes all of us, and the universe, spiritually well. There is sacrifice in connection with this as we will give up our religions, their dogmas, and outdated patriarchal traditions.

Natural disasters are clearing more and more negativity, and the more the human race works together, the more it also clears the negative energy throughout the Earth plane.

This book is written in a conventional way so readers can gain a clear understanding of what is written. People will awaken to the information and will think about the spiritual meaning of life. If people stopped and thought from a spiritual point of view, they could apply this new information to what they believe in, to have stronger thoughts of spirituality that are essential to keep them on track to a better outcome that is advisable for the Age of Aquarius. People are evolving by connecting through spirituality together, mentally, with their spiritual thoughts and way of thinking, rather than being separate, to connect their consciousness more and to be in alignment with the new age spiritual way of living.

As we keep moving forward with spirituality, the leaders, presenting themselves very tactfully, will lead the citizens in cooperation. The leaders are going out at large from the community to have full scale cooperation truly incorporated into our spirituality. They will fully cover the need for timely and prompt organising of the citizens to proceed with agreeing to work together for the better, for an extreme spiritual outcome. The organisation of everyone participating will have pleasing results, from the law of cause and effect (what you cause, do or say affects you) in action, so that what we work out together comes back to us tenfold, with an ongoing domino effect.

The reality is that people are turning to learning, as they comprehend that with everything coming together, and with the expansion of the state of wellbeing, that their understanding is biased towards their own wellbeing. Your preconceived opinions that once determined your first thoughts are now changed and are quite different as a result of all the new knowledge, facts and proof that has been given to you by official public announcements and other sources of factual information, giving you a thorough hold of a whole new age of spirituality. Community meetings that are being held prompt people to get together to make agreements, and this automatically has spirituality involved, even though they may not be aware of it.

Fluctuations in the world with continual ups and downs caused by confusion, where it seems like things are getting better, then it seems like they are getting worse, then it seems like they are getting better, and so on, can be deceiving, as it appears things are not improving. People comprehend that it is conceivable that they will have the privilege of living in the newer world when the confusion is out of the way. Eliminating confusion makes it easier to receive a higher standard of consciousness, that drives communication between us to gain the understanding that is needed for our connection. What we enjoy, we have mindfulness with, and that makes learning much more fun and exciting as we are focusing on the good, in contrast to the bad things happening on Earth.

Ladders are an extreme sign of connection in many different ways. In the material world ladders represent the spiritual world, with the climb, and the movement up the ladder by people who are gaining meaning from all the knowledge that they integrate into themselves, through their learning and understanding, due to this connection.

A free thinker, such as myself, loves the knowledge and learning about logic, through the perception of my own thinking and faith in what I am doing. The procedure of the learning process will put those people who are newly involved, into the connection of ladders and spirituality.

Agnostics are people with a good attitude and logical thinking, whilst keeping their own freedom of thought and knowing, and they have a core issue of neither believing nor disbelieving what is beyond the physical world.

Freedom is important to us. We want personal freedom in our own lives, and we want freedom in the world for everyone else as well, and we want lasting freedom that endures, that is standard worldwide, the same for everyone. When we have open freedom we can think more, which focuses our minds on ladders into spirituality better. Freedom overrides the counterattack from negativity in every one of the subjects in these chapters, so that the negative side of each subject is put aside, and then we can see what is needed for a positive outcome. We have the capability to put negativity out of the way to get a good outcome.

Realisation about ladders may come out in your dreams, by giving you messages regarding what to do. Dreaming of ladders can be very positive as it signifies a higher connection with the spiritual realm, and it can have enormous impact upon your control of your life here in the material world. Emotions and actions in your dreaming are out of your control, but if you have a bad dream, it can cause you to wake up. The content of good dreams often awakens you to new knowledge that shows you the pathway to follow, including what you need, and what the outcome is.

The ladder must be put on a stable surface and be handled correctly for safety reasons so that it may be climbed safely. Your own intuition may help you know how stable and safe it is.

Dreams do have powerful meanings, so a dream of falling off a ladder could be a warning sign to be careful with ladders in real life. Ladders are hazardous, and a fall will serve to remind you to keep yourself safe and secure. Always be aware in your mind that a positive ambitious attitude will make your climb up the ladder stronger, and you will not have to worry about falling or broken bones. Clearly you have the strength to climb higher without any fear, therefore you may push yourself upwards right to the top to get the highest benefit of spirituality. Each step you take as you go up is more overwhelming, and with each step you are getting wiser, which is what is meant for you. This is all truth, and you would only question it if you thought you would not be able to do it.

It may always be straightforward in a fair manner for you, working through what you have to do, with your essence, on your pathway in life, but you may not want others to interfere in your outcome and in what you are doing, as it is personal to you with your own essence.

There is an imaginary circle that becomes more real with your thoughts and the detail you put into it, that has a circumference around the outside of it, and a center-point of intelligence inside the circle. If you look into the center of the circle, you can see the intelligence that we are all working towards, with our connection, and what we are all doing together. The circumference and the circle is the energy of everything that happens on Earth, and what all the people who are involved in this, are doing. The circle shows the intelligence of us working together, and the center point is where we collect knowledge from the 100% intelligence there, so we can see what to do, while the outside of the circle is imaginary. Laddering into spirituality brings you ultimately to the center of the circle, the center mark of intelligence (at the top of the ladder), and then you are in alignment and moving away from religion, to be involved in the new age.

You will always certainly have a safe pathway with your ladder. You can overcome heights and feel secure, and you will be able to be more evolved and investigating spirituality more.

If the ladder breaks in your dreams, you will not fall from it or hurt yourself, as it just means that you have a few issues to resolve, and even if they are not positive issues, when there is no fear, they can easily be dealt with and done away with. It can be exciting to remember and even keep records of your dreams, and you can then form positive affirmations from them, which can lead to you moving ahead and doing what you want to do in your life. Often people cannot remember their dreams when they wake up in the morning, although sometimes they can remember if it was good or bad, but not what it was about, and that is natural and happens to many people, including myself.

If you are always gripping onto a ladder and are unable to even move slowly up it anymore, this is a sign that you should climb back down the ladder and look back over your dream records for any signs or synchronicities (meaningful coincidences) to become aware that something is not quite right. You can then deal with it by forcing yourself to face up to the issue and then focus on resolving it. Your dreams, whether involving any ladder capability or not, are always there for you to notice the signs and to interpret, and by collecting your dream interpretations and making sense of them, to see what is right.

Different types of ladders can have a big impact and play an enormous part. Let us look now at what the ladder is made of. Having a wooden ladder to walk up, for instance, can have the meaning to be more grounded, stable and centered in your mind and body. A metal ladder is associated with a strong yearning for growth and fulfilment in your life and career, and this has a lot of impact. You could rise to a higher status of professionalism in your career involving more prosperity and teamwork.

Your dreams about ladders support you, when it is the perfect time, to climb to the highest part of the ladder to gain a higher spiritual outcome in the real world. This will enhance your self-esteem as you are climbing, and once you arrive at the top you will feel the achievement. Every thought that you think after the outcome has happened helps you to discover spirituality and see that every action has a motion that creates the outcome. A firm belief in ladders into spirituality gives you the perspective to fulfil, in the right timing, the outcome that you know is right and appropriate for yourself.

Religious people will go further into spirituality when the religions are eliminated worldwide, and they will have the ladder to incorporate into their new beliefs.

Everything we have talked about so far is about being able to combine things, and if we can combine everything, with solutions to all the obstacles listed in the chapter titles of this book, there will be a forceful universal expansion on Earth with an outcome that is for the better.

Those who identify with spirituality and the truth inside themselves in their core (as their identity), are those who think for themselves and who have ongoing learning about spirituality, and also religious people whose religion has been eliminated, because of the conflicts that have had a big effect but did not get people anywhere.

The inner talk that you have with yourself regarding your learning is moving you to a higher level, due to the information, and what you understand from it, that you have gained from sources such as this book. It is like a conveyor belt that automatically goes up with every sentence you read, as the author and the reader can both understand the connection at a much faster rate of spirituality, although I know at first you may well need to compromise. The movement of the conveyor belt is similar to the movement of spirituality going up the ladder.

I write this book about what I know, in order to give people information that I know may help them, as I know what is really inside myself.

How do I know all this? I went to a 'Journey' practitioner, who was a hypnotherapist, and from this I discovered who I am and what my life's purpose is.

I am truly peace, and that lasts for eternity, as my life's purpose is to learn and give eternal peace.

Putting all the facts together in this book was the best way for me to explain the concepts that I am interpreting from my own self, and to get the message across to readers. It depends on the readers' interpretation and understanding of these writings and what they want to get from it. It is important to me to write this book so that I can get my true essence across, and so I can fully enjoy life and feel whole inside.

The ability that I have is to communicate my perceptions of what is right for your understanding, that is right for what you need to see, so that you can figure out what to translate from your ingrained beliefs (religion) into exceptional spirituality. This is confined to how you can change your perspective to what you can live with, being the perspective of what you can see in the new age spirituality compared to what has been eliminated from religion, so that you can change over and become ingrained in the new spirituality that is perfect for you.

The truth is within you, and you will not feel fully whole until you understand and know what is really inside you. Know that you will be able to translate from your religion through to spirituality without any trouble. Religion will automatically disappear over time as people are letting go of it and thinking more for themselves. Fewer and fewer people will believe in religion and more and more people will incorporate spirituality into their minds and daily living.

Some people who are not fulfilled by spirituality are not really open to knowing about it, but I certainly have proof that people can change just from the things I am writing about in this book. Even the non-believers or atheists pray in a time of crisis; they cannot help themselves. Perhaps sometimes it might be that atheists, especially those that are complete narcissists, are purposely put into a crisis situation that is bad enough that they have to cry for help and are forced to pray for security, so they can get back on track in their life. Many of us (including myself) have heard stories about the presence of spirits or maybe guardian angels keeping people safe and alive.

Some people have had near-death experiences that have changed their thinking and beliefs, and, whether they are atheists, agnostics or religious, the outcome of their near-death experience depends on what they perceive and go through, and what happens, and also what messages they receive and bring back with them.

I have never been very spiritual, as I have always had the view that we do not know what is beyond our physical world. This is called

Agnosticism, which is the name given to it by an English biologist some time ago in the past, and many people have used this term since then.

The more inclined we are to know exactly what is bringing the two worlds together, the more that the help of everyone working together will be enough to bring world peace, and the joy of all that. Enlightenment is incredibly powerful when connecting the two worlds together, giving a sense of wellbeing through the connection to spirituality.

Organisation plays a big role in our material world, as well as in the spiritual world. You have a bond with both worlds when you know them both, and this understanding makes your communication with everybody far better.

Let us now return to ladders. We have learned how to operate with them, and also their beneficial effects, but there is still more to know. We will look at colours of ladders now and the significance that this has. Colours have powerful meanings, and they have just as much impact as the type of ladder it is. The brighter the colour, the more impact it has with vitality and success. Red, orange, green, yellow and blue are colours that your ladder in your dream could be. Spiritual guides give the ladder in your dream a certain colour according to the message they want to give you. Dreaming is spiritual, and spiritual guides put information into your dream to influence your thinking and behaviour, to help you progress as you are supposed to in the material world. Our dreaming gives us strength, supported by our spirit guides, and inspires us, so that we know how to proceed in our lives from the messages we receive, and we feel the connection with spirituality, to have wellbeing in our everyday living and move on in our lives here in the physical world.

The best ladder, that you can accomplish the most with, is the golden ladder. There is nothing that can beat gold; it is the most powerful element, and if you dream about a golden ladder lengthening your life, then you have the ability to bring that into your reality. It gives you the ability to expand to your true potential and be highly vitalised for obtaining your wishes and your purpose. This is possible by aligning your thoughts with your wishes, and controlling and watching your thoughts, to keep them positive, as the universe reflects back to you 100% of what you put out in the energy of your thoughts, and that is guaranteed. You will receive the rewards and benefits of your actions when you reframe your thoughts to be positive and to give you the stability to manifest what you wish for, with the automatic support of the universe. You will recognise the unfolding of your wishes. It will seem as if your life has fast forwarded, as the benefits of fulfilment play out in your life, feeling like you have twice the potential within yourself.

For those who migrate to the new higher level that has a new outcome, it will take time to adjust, and although they will be full of enthusiasm, things can seem topsy-turvy, and they want to get things right and diffuse the confusion. At the crossroads turnover point it is confusing at first, and it will take a little while to adjust, but then confusion becomes far less. To help out more with this, you can breathe deeply in and out to release tension and stress. The more deep breathing you do, and the releasing of the rubbish inside you, the more you will be working for spirituality on Earth and healing bad karma. Being grounded and centered in your body and on the Earth plane, and being focused, helps to heal wounds by planting new seeds, and gives you the capacity to live through what you need to.

The more people that migrate into the new world the less confusion there will be, as the migrants will find that the government's curriculum is well thought out and special. This is because it has been incorporated with the information from the children that were newborn from the spiritual world, to guide and direct how things should be organised in the material world for our spiritual wellbeing in the new age.

The next generation of children will be our teachers, and they will have the power as they are born into the new Age of Aquarius, and they will teach us, the adults. People will know this and will know they have to listen to the children. Adults will be able to incorporate new age rights into law through the government, from what the children are teaching us, as there will be a much stronger democracy. In the new age we can work in with the government better and it will not be so hard to do.

When we work together well on the Earth plane, it automatically creates a dome of energy over us, making us more grounded and aligned. The dome shape is amazing; it is the same shape as the Earth, and it ingrains us firmly into the Earth to move forward with spirituality. The energy dome lifts us up and protects us, and keeps our physical body aligned, centered and grounded. When we are centered we are balanced and calm in our body, mind and spirit, and we manage our emotions. Being grounded is being stable, sensible and realistic, and making good decisions.

By now your mind is familiar with the things I am writing about, so that you could make a resolution to fulfil the purpose of your essence and the Earth's essence right through to the new age. You will know your essence, because we are all connected, when we all work together for the new world, as this Earth's essence is to have world peace. All the information is being poured into you when you go to learn and work with others towards redevelopment, which comprises of spirituality with a resolution for the goal of world peace.

By taking part and focusing on what you are doing, and taking notes of your daily progress, you will find it worthwhile and enjoyable. If others are still having conflicts, then it is their stuff for them to deal with. You may influence others in a good way by focusing consistently on what you are doing, so that, after a while, those who are doing negative things may click on to this and decide to follow your example.

I believe that people need to listen to the information in these writings and be open to finding the solution to having the spirituality that we are all waking up to.

Any worries or fears involving money that you may have that puts pressure on you, may be released by breathing deeply and long, to make the brain feel stress-free, and to have the stamina to participate with others. As we are all acting unitedly for peace by guiding each other along, the universe will create and support miracles, giving us a new logical understanding of the new age. As you continue on, you automatically follow the guidance to be active and take action for a peaceful world.

CHAPTER 8

GENDER, SEXISM AND HOMOPHOBIA

There are two genders, male and female, which are necessary to reproduce to keep the human species going. Sexism is when there is discrimination on the basis of gender. Homophobia is the fear of homosexuals, and hostility towards them, often because of religion.

Our attitudes, beliefs and behaviours are commonly inherited from our parents and relatives, with influence from friends and religious teachings, and are drummed into us when we are growing up.

There are also transsexuals, who change their gender to the opposite gender by having medical procedures. In some cultures, there is debate about this and discrimination, as many, especially those with strong religious beliefs, cannot accept transgender people and believe there should only be two genders, male and female.

There are a lot of issues between the male and female genders due to gender conflicts, with females wanting to have equal rights and equal opportunities with males. Many men do not want this, as they want to be dominant and controlling, and they see women as inferior to themselves.

Homosexuality is a big issue in many countries, particularly those with strict religious attitudes and religious leaders in government.

Through the generations things have improved, with attitudes rising higher, old beliefs being let go, and humans starting to think for themselves instead of continuing to believe the things they were taught in their childhood. Things have changed a lot from when our grandparents were young.

Let us look at gender and spirituality now. The majority of humans, whether they are religious or spiritual, have always believed that God is a super-human male being who lives in the kingdom of heaven up in the sky, and who has all the same judgemental attitudes, hates and prejudices that humans have. This is exactly what has caused so much fear in us. Would a loving god really want to punish people? Religious believers say "yes". Spiritualists may have an easier understanding. Spirits on the other side in heaven/the afterlife, keep their same gender, looks and personality only for the purpose of being recognised by their family members. Those who die naturally of old age looking frail and wrinkled and in bad health, may present themselves as in their thirties, for instance, when they looked young and healthy.

Religious leaders preach about sin in order to use fear to have power and control over the population. In early times religious scriptures were changed to manipulate the citizenry through fear, to keep them in narrow rigid gender roles in society. This rubbish is no longer needed in contemporary times, as it is holding back peace.

As we realise the truth of why we are here and the truth of our reality, it changes the way we think and what we do, and we recognise that we need to rely on each other and join together to work things out for a better outcome.

If God has no gender and is just pure energy that is connected to everything, being 100% whole, then that means that we are all God! All the 'Journey' work that I did with my 'Journey' practitioner made me realise that I am connected to everything through my own true essence.

We must have both genders in the material world for life to exist. If reincarnation is real, then it means that more souls keep being reincarnated so that they can learn more life lessons or experience the things on Earth that their soul wants them to experience. There are very many souls in the spiritual world who have often had lives on other planets, perhaps even in other galaxies, or other universes. Our universe is massive, and there are other universes beyond ours, so there is plenty of room in the spiritual world for all souls. A lot of souls have lives on Earth as it is a difficult place where a lot of lessons can be learned. In recent times humanity is evolving more, and you can have more struggles and learning to strengthen your soul. There is a lot of karma with learning lessons; 'what goes around comes around' is a well-known saying. If men are mean to women they may have to reincarnate as a woman and be treated badly by men, and vice versa. Sexism must surely be a karmic issue, whether it was in this incarnation or another. Sometimes people can be judgemental and accuse others of being sexist when they were not trying to be sexist at all; this can cause trouble when people have different impressions, and different interpretations of others' actions.

Heterosexuality is when we are attracted to the opposite gender, and this has always been seen as normal. This is in the Bible. Ingrained beliefs that man is made for woman has caused tremendous stress to homosexuals, because of homophobia. Homosexuality cannot be helped; it happens naturally and is more common than society generally thinks. Estimations are that 10% of the population is 'gay'. In the same way, heterosexuality also occurs naturally without you choosing it. Strict religious believers think homosexuals must have treatment to force them to be heterosexual.

These days things are changing; the old attitudes are being questioned more, and there is greater understanding and caring. Change will continue until there is extreme change, or transformation, for the better. One day the world will be totally accepting of homosexuality, and it will be wholly understood that there is nothing wrong with it, thereby eradicating homophobia. Heterosexuality and homosexuality will be treated equally, and people will realise that it feels normal to be homosexual and to be attracted to the same gender. When people accept others' differences, that is when things really start unfolding for world peace.

Let us look at masculinity and feminism now. There can be a lot of controversy about this. Women want equal rights with men and to be treated equally, so that they can do as much as men do. Masculinity is about male roles and behaviours; and about maintaining their dominance over females. Bad behaviours can include selfishness and out-of-control violence and abuse of their power over women. An alternative action that can take place is for males to use their power for good, by treating women well and protecting and safeguarding them to give them security.

The new era, with the universe supporting us, has the ability to automatically shift people's beliefs so they can form new attitudes. The outcome of this is forgiveness between men and women and enhancement of gender equality so that we can have peace. Nothing can beat the power of the universe; it is powerful and 100% whole, and it supports us beneficially and creates miracles.

Feminine energy is becoming stronger, and we have a greater knowledge and understanding that women are now leading with the power that they have in the governments. We have some women presidents and prime ministers, who have powerful positions. The behavioural status is changing, and we enjoy seeing this. There are a growing number of men that are changing their attitudes and supporting women, and this balances things more between the genders. When women protest and push for their rights, it creates greater financial balance between the two genders, and once this equality of income is guaranteed, then the division and power struggle between the genders may end. When they feel that there is fairness, it creates additional unity between them to work together peacefully.

Let us take a step back now and bring together all we have learned about gender and sexism, as this confrontational energy plays a big part in society. With 100% understanding, issues around gender and sexism will become a thing of the past, and there will be respect between the genders with no sexism. New thinking on the behaviour and attitudes towards gender, sexism and homosexuality will take place, leading to the elimination of homophobia. It will be realised clearly that homosexuality is totally fine; we will not have any worries about it, and it will be as good as heterosexuality. It will be understood that love in any true way is exceptionally valuable.

As we move further into the spiritual brotherhood of the new age, the acceptance of homosexuality will grow increasingly, creating a domino effect which will seem miraculous to people as they will not be expecting it.

Everything is connected, and if we can understand that, then all faiths/religions give way to that which brings us together spiritually.

If we know that God has no gender and is just the awesome power of everything that is whole, well then, it automatically balances the male and female energies to work together for the healing of bad karma. Seeing gender in a new way and knowing we will be moving into a new world that is beyond belief, will bring us unity.

CHAPTER 9

POVERTY, POLLUTION AND DISEASE

Poverty, pollution and disease are huge problems on Earth, affecting the health of a big percentage of the population. If we were able to solve these issues and be free from them, life on Earth would be much healthier.

Although there have been advances in using non-polluting energies, which are far healthier for human life and for the planet, the big oil companies keep fighting back strongly as they want to continue making a lot of money. They will never willingly stop drilling for oil, and they work against the introduction of non-polluting energy to ensure that there is no competition that would lower their lucrative income from oil. Eventually the oil available for drilling from inside the Earth will run out, but the oil companies want to make big money for as long as they can.

Pollution and also climate change, whether you believe in it or not, are causing concern, and government leaders have regular meetings at which they make agreements to reduce the levels of pollutants in each country. Big companies who are polluting fight back stealthily to keep control of the power they have, so they can keep producing their goods and keep their large incomes. The annual agreements that governments make to reduce pollution require cutting back on the causes within a certain number of years - five, ten or more years in the future, but we really need to do this much sooner, like right now!

In cities, because there are a lot of vehicles, factories and industries, there is air pollution that leads to health issues, as those who live there do not have fresh air to breathe. The use of fossil fuels, coal, oil and gas, is hard to stop and must be regulated by law to make changes mandatory. It can take a long time to change things when powerful companies do not want to change. An imbalance on the Earth plane is brought about by drilling for oil and burning fossil fuels, that not only cause pollution but also the greenhouse gases that are of great concern.

However, over time things do change and new developments and technology such as electric vehicles are produced. When consumers buy these new products in increasing numbers it helps to change things. Alternative forms of energy are becoming more accepted in our daily lives such as solar power and wind turbines, which are natural energies. If solar energy, that is free to use, is incorporated into all areas of our daily living, the next generation of children will live in a healthier world. It is easier to use the sun rather than building wind turbines that take up land space and need the right amount of wind energy to operate.

In the future we will be able to use ocean water for water-powered machinery and for drinking, as there will be a way to dissolve the salt and pollution out of seawater. When vehicles are powered by other forms of energy the oil companies will not make the same level of income as before, and when they are no longer making a fortune and thriving, they will give up on their business and start something new.

The middle eastern countries are big oil producers. For example, Qatar is extremely wealthy from selling oil even though they are only a small country. Because of the money they make they have a lot of power and do not stop producing oil. When electric vehicles and other new developments increase, the oil producers cannot keep selling the same amount of oil. The continuing process of using alternative energy sources is ideal for reducing oil production, which is a healthier state of living, with fresh air to breathe. We will feel much cleaner when maximum cooperation takes place to destroy pollutants and toxins.

In the future people will not litter as they will be brought up to be healthier, with new laws so that you will be fined if you are caught littering. Individuals will be far more cautious about what they put in their bodies. For instance, they will not smoke tobacco; it will be a thing of the past. Tobacco smoke has been a cause of cancer for a long time.

Members of society are rethinking and realising their old ways of thinking are no longer relevant and are not solving the issues they are concerned about. The younger ones of the new generation coming in have a higher awareness of things, as they are born into the new era of Aquarius and are more advanced in their thinking, to make the moves necessary for big changes. These young people can see that what has been tried so far has not worked nearly enough. They will be our teachers; they will activate changes with the older people. The new generation of younger people now being incarnated on Earth will bring in the new frequency that will make the Earth lighter and brighter for us to live in, and that we will gain from.

Support for global changes regarding pollution, poverty and disease will come from democratic countries and the United Nations in New York, to make beneficial changes for the better. Pollution will be reduced when governments meet together amicably and make important agreements. The Age of Aquarius supports this government interaction.

Writings such as in this book are progressive and have the ability to change interpretations, cause rethinking and do away with confusion. People will understand that there is hope that the future will settle down.

Government schemes for pollution will actualise. Environmental activists will have no worries as agreements will be made to dissolve the dirtiness of pollution. With everyone's support pollution will keep being reduced, until the Earth is completely clean.

Poverty is widespread on Earth with a wide gap between rich and poor countries and individuals. Ill-health, disease and deaths that could be preventable are the result of lack of adequate food and healthcare for those living in poverty. Many richer citizens do care about the injustices of poverty and disease but do not have the power or authority to take action. There has always been brutal poverty, and it has been widely reported in the news media. But because the public do not realise that we are all connected and are one with all things, as there is no reporting about this, they do not know what to do about poverty, so they do nothing.

Goods will be exported to other countries, to share, when we learn to care for each other. When this support and caring by citizens happens, the universe will automatically support us right back, so that everyone will have enough income to eradicate poverty. Agreements will be needed for this to happen, between the governments of the rich and poor countries, to put new systems and order into place to bring health and wellbeing by working together. Their standpoint must be to meet halfway in between, to cooperate, with sharing. Agreements must be valued and adhered to, and the actions carried out must be watched and inspected to ensure the goods are being shared with those who need them. It must be realised that supervision and control of the sharing and distribution is needed.

Those who are poor will be happy with the benefits of clean and healthy everyday living that they receive from the support of rich countries. It takes effort for humans to share, even when agreements have been made to share goods with other countries, but this always helps to firstly reduce, and then cure, poverty.

When society perceives that we are all one, we will feel the connection that makes us joyous, and will know we have to help others out, thus making Earth a more enjoyable place to live. The universe notices our happier status, as we are working together, and supports us with even stronger cures and remedies for poverty and disease.

In the countries where there is the direst poverty, large numbers of vulnerable people die from starvation and disease, but when those with the means and resources to help know that we are all connected, this will turn things around to remedy poverty and disease at a much faster rate. The material world and everyone living on it are more important than money. Money causes the chaos of greediness.

Once we all comprehend the oneness connection, we will finally come to know exactly how to cure poverty, disease and pollution, and this will be much healthier for all human beings and the material world. There will be enough money to cure poverty worldwide. We will give to others by exporting goods, to make life happier for everyone, including those currently living in poverty.

CHAPTER 10

NATURAL DISASTERS

Natural disasters have always occurred on Earth. However, in recent times these have become more frequent and severe, affecting a greater number of humans. Some of the natural disasters that have a major effect on human society are earthquakes, hurricanes (also known as tropical cyclones and typhoons in some areas of the world), floods, landslides, wildfires, severe winter weather (including blizzards and storms), volcanic eruptions, tsunamis, tornadoes, droughts, heat waves and avalanches.

Why are these occurring more often?

If we consider hurricanes, which appear to be growing larger in size, stronger in category and more frequent during the hurricane season, the scientific data states that the greenhouse gas effect is warming ocean temperatures globally. Increasing levels of greenhouse gases such as carbon dioxide and methane in the Earth's atmosphere will lead to rising ocean water temperatures, in turn creating fiercer hurricanes.

From a spiritual point of view, major hurricanes and other big natural disasters cleanse the negativity on the Earth. They are a wake-up call to bring humans together. In serious situations where residents are trapped in their homes in a natural disaster tragedy, and they cry for help, but cannot get it, they often lose their lives because of the flood, earthquake, hurricane, landslide, etc. That is a sign that humans need to be better organised with the purpose of helping each other.

Natural disasters keep happening because there is so much negative energy building up on Earth, for example, the confusion in the fourth dimension with the tragedies of wars, etc. They will continue occurring until the Earth plane is cleansed. The more that humans keep fighting, the more natural disasters the Earth has to have to cleanse itself.

When natural disasters and their recovery cleanup is over, helpers return to their normal lives of not helping others. Therefore, more natural disasters need to happen to keep those people helping, also to make them aware of the dangers and that they must unite to overcome tragedies. This creates good karmic energy. When we have more knowledge and understanding about coming together in every aspect of life, then life will lead us on to having peace within ourselves. Once we all have internal peace inside us, then because our reality goes out from us in our thoughts and energy, this creates a peaceful world.

Natural disasters will maintain their repeated ferocious frequency until we have proof of our connection of oneness between us all. This is guaranteed to help. Extreme natural disasters generate fears of doomsday, but what they actually give us is a strong message of truth to move forward and help each other out. There will still be extensive coverage of ongoing natural disasters until we come to terms with the real reasons why they are occurring, and how to stop them. It will be understood how to work through them and survive them by developing skills to do so, and by making it harder or even impossible for them to happen, once we have the knowledge. We will all learn the meaning of natural disasters and have the understanding of how they form, so that clear calculations will be made to know what we can do about it. We will be moving ahead and without a doubt Mother Nature will throw her force at us again to wake us up and keep us active to heal the planet. We have always got her as our wake-up call, to clear negativity and bring us together.

Let us look now at Mother Nature. She does her duty through the profusion of destruction that causes upheaval to humans, using natural forces in the rapid growth of disaster after disaster. Mother Nature is often seen as not being real but can seem real to some people as they believe it has a spirit that releases its tremendous force when necessary to maintain the tension it holds. The name Mother Nature can be very powerfully identifying, and people relate to this name according to how they see things.

Humans worry that a natural disaster will happen in their area and affect them, and they wonder what will happen next, fearing the worst. The worst-case scenarios are when residents are completely trapped and cannot escape, for example when a deluge of torrential rainfall causes floods. The only way they will survive is if emergency services help them, but when the disaster is so atrocious help does not reach everyone, or in time. The way forward is to just keep hoping that severe natural disasters that cause destruction will not happen again. Moving onward we understand that coming together will heal the negative energy that we put out on Earth, so that serious and damaging natural disasters may be eliminated.

The worst natural disaster that I have experienced personally was the serious earthquake and aftershocks in the city of Christchurch, New Zealand in 2010 and 2011, when I was living there. After the two biggest quakes in September 2010 and February 2011, there were a large number of aftershocks for a long time afterwards. These were frightening for me, and I felt unsafe. It is a feeling of helplessness and having no control and not knowing what to do. One day, in 2012, when there were still aftershocks, a well-known psychic medium from overseas visited Christchurch to offer healing to those affected by the quakes, and to the Earth. She sent pure love into the ground to heal it. This shows how a gifted psychic can have the love for humanity and the planet and use healing power to create healing. It proves that we can do it too by learning to love and care for one another more. We will make forward progress on natural disasters that are happening and that are so powerful they are beyond our control.

The more we learn about natural disasters, and the deeper connection with understanding that we have with others, then our task is to conquer the disasters and be protected from them so we can farewell the past and all its natural disasters and the way humans have treated each other so badly. The way onward into our future is knowing that the elimination of fear is ongoing and controllable. There is no need for fear in the future because there will not be anything that causes us to be fearful.

The advantage of natural disasters is that they cleanse the planet energetically. Disadvantages are the dangers to human life and property. The pressure of the Earth withholds its tension, and when it gets too much to cope with, it has to have natural disasters at extreme force as a release. The pressure within us human beings to understand about natural disasters is very strong. There are a lot of different interpretations and different ways of seeing things according to individual beliefs and ways of thinking.

Snow is cleansing as it falls, and snowflakes are gentle and pretty and have a healing effect on nature's energy. Avalanches are a real concern in the Spring in certain places when the snow softens and is loose for possible collapse and downward fall as an avalanche. Climate change is happening in all ways according to people's thoughts and ways of thinking and what they are expecting, for example, some people believe in global warming, some believe in global cooling, and so on. But people have to progress and have to realise that although natural disasters are happening, this is to cleanse negative energy out so we can move ahead. All natural disasters are bringing us forward to connect to the higher dimension.

People form their own beliefs, according to their own way of thinking, about the topics covered in the chapters of this book. The way to follow through is to go with the information in this book and also the outside coverage by the news media and what they anticipate will happen from their own coverage that they do. The one thing that we really do not want in the new world is for anything to happen that creates negative energy. Recurring natural disasters interrupt peace and prevent the containment of calmness in the new golden Age of Aquarius. The world would still have to release negativity, which is what we want to be done with, so that no further natural disasters occur. Our world will be a much better place, and we will evolve in more ways when natural disasters are reduced to a normal non-destructive level that we are comfortable with as they are minor, and the destructive ones are eliminated.

As we all come into the new Age of Aquarius, we will have the same understanding of things as everyone else, as we will have full connection with them. Our acquaintances will come out to help and will have the knowledge to support us into Aquarius. We will stay on the same timeline and work things out by working through it all together. As we move further into the new age, we will know more about universal love, and this becomes a part of our life, making us much more caring and able to release our own negative karmic energy so there will be no need for natural disasters.

Earth's atmosphere will show the results of the cleansing, and we will know it has happened as the air will feel much fresher to breathe.

Earthquakes, where buildings collapse and cause deaths, compel inhabitants to realise they must work together. Memorial services one year later, and similar events, have a big healing effect on the Earth and brings the community together. They know that increasing their efforts to work things out may prevent other disasters from happening. Powerful hurricanes are costly, and society joins forces to repair the damage and rebuild. Forest fires are destructive to the forest and properties, but they cleanse the negativity. Fighting the fires is a lot of work for firefighters with hoses, helicopters and monsoon buckets. The old forest is burned, but a new forest eventually grows, and there is a healing effect on the atmosphere.

Everything that is happening with climate change is either agreeable or disagreeable to people, depending on how they see it. Global warming or cooling (as some believe it is time for the next ice age) has a big impact on people's set beliefs. Some just believe that the climate is changing, with topsy-turvy seasons, and the weather being all over the place, inconsistent and erratic.

After Earth's destructive natural disasters are eliminated, there will still be minor disasters, and these are acceptable. When realisation comes to people and they understand connection, they recognise that natural disasters are actually man-made from our negativity. They realise that the releasing that is done through natural disasters only has to happen until all karmic energy has dissolved. When humans come to terms with the spirituality of the fifth dimension, they will comprehend why the extreme forces of natural disasters happened in the third and fourth dimensions, and they will understand about the cleansing.

In the new age we will be pleased that we have been brought together by the cleansing of the natural disasters. We will not believe how we used to treat others during the old Age of Pisces, and we will remember the extreme weather and enormous natural disasters that brought us all together. We will keep going and survive living through the disasters to move to the new Earth. Natural disasters shake us all up and bring us together to help out and care. They wake us up, and the more severe they are, the more we have to help each other. Severe regular natural disasters stick in people's minds and memories. Any disaster can have danger, therefore, we know we have to work hard on trying to stick together. There could be unknown dangers, and we have to stay together to protect the Earth and ensure that the build-up of negative energy does not cause the Earth to collapse and be destroyed.

We will protect our planet, and life will always go on, as we know it has to for human beings to survive. When fear is released and natural disasters are eliminated as negativity is dissolved, there will be no further danger. This will proceed very quickly when we have the knowledge of why natural disaster phenomena occurs. When this proof is known there will be no doubts, just ongoing progress.

CHAPTER 11

RACE AND CULTURE

Conflicts between different races and cultures on Earth have existed right back to ancient times. In human society, it is generally said that those who look differently from us with different skin colour and facial features are of a different race from us. In the past, the original indigenous inhabitants of each country or continent were all of different races.

Today in our modern world with immigration, refugees and travel, large numbers of people have moved from their original homeland where they were born, to other countries in the hope of having a better life with more prosperity. This has resulted in many countries now having a mixture of quite a few races who brought with them their customs, culture, religions and attitudes. Because their culture is part of their identity, they continue their traditions rather than suddenly changing to the culture and attitudes of their new homeland to assimilate and blend in. These countries have ended up with more than one race and culture, creating an adjustment for the existing population who may find it disruptive in their once uniform society and lives. It creates the need for racial tolerance and acceptance of others who look different and have a different way of living, with different religions and attitudes. Prejudice and discrimination against those who are of a different race and culture can cause upheaval, tension, and in some cases, violence.

The members of a racial group who have migrated to another country, and perhaps their descendants as well, often tend to stick together in their own groups and live in the same areas, as this gives them a feeling of familiarity, comfort and safety, and a sense of belonging. They can feel unwelcome mingling with those who already lived there, who are of a different race from them, and may not feel overly accepted or included.

People of different races may feel they have little in common with each other, so they do not make the effort to get to know others. New immigrants may not speak the language of their new country well, or may wear very different clothing, such as head coverings that women in some religions are made to wear by their menfolk and male religious leaders as an act of oppression and dominance over them. Locals can feel that the immigrants are just too different from themselves and are bringing in customs that they dislike, or feel are wrong or offensive. Locals may not understand the different behaviour or why they are behaving differently, and they cannot adjust to it.

Citizens do not always want immigrants with very different cultures and behaviours coming to their country in large numbers and changing their society, and changing what they feel is the identity of their country. The effort of tolerating big differences can be stressful.

The spiritual purpose of immigration that mixes people of different races and cultures in the same country, is so that people will be forced to learn tolerance and learn to live side by side without discord, strife or disharmony. It may take many years to learn to accept each other, and this may not happen until the following generations, being the children and grandchildren of the immigrants, go to school together, play together, and accept one another.

We have to think clearly about discrimination and the way we are treating people. When we deal with the conflicts there will be more balance and harmony between races and cultures. There must be fairness, commitment and togetherness as we keep moving ahead together. As we yearn to get things right for world peace, forgiveness and commitment will lead to a high standard of working together with high achievement. We are going to be purposefully on track with the new mindset needed to keep things intact, supposedly with what is meant to be done, and we will feel alive knowing what is ahead of us, including having compassion towards one another. We will feel and have the composition (the formation) of our awareness as it is activated throughout the universe and by authorities on Earth. Congratulations are due as we move up to the higher frequencies of the fifth dimension where we all discover the flow that gives us joy, and not just that, but also to be living fully in a world of peace and harmony.

From all the conflicts, we have been pulled downwards, so we feel we have not achieved anything; we feel neglected and not listened to. Developing new communication skills will prevent us continuing downwards. Social skills are important to get to know each other better and integrate new ways of communicating that are enjoyable. We are yearning for races and cultures to thrive and to be enjoying each other and collaborating. As we learn more about races and cultures, we will have no doubt that we can learn from each other. It is like there is a labelled prescription at the center of the universe saying:

'Understand me and work with me for world peace'. All races and cultures need to adhere to a standardised list of rules for behaviour and wellbeing to be able to create togetherness. It is essential to us to have that standard of remembrance of our oneness connection to live upon. The beauty of togetherness is that we form relationships with each other, which enables better organisation for cooperating and performing our duty to get on together, as though we are having an apprenticeship with each other in human society. All races need to come together and have racial tolerance so they can live amongst each other in peace. The power of the universe and people's tolerance will deliberately force people to be accepting of all races.

There have been films and movies made to make us think about racial tolerance. Races must have tolerance to go into the new world; their behaviours will become more acceptable to each other, as because of their new understanding and realisation, they will change their cultural behaviours that were unacceptable. The strong expectation of tolerance is fair, but there cannot be tolerance with all the confusion in the world preventing it. 'Crash' was the 2004 movie that has a theme of racial tolerance. Set in Los Angeles, the movie shows the racial prejudices of the characters, who belong to several different races, and how their lives are affected when a series of negative events take place involving vehicles, crimes and confrontations, where they have to help each other.

In the future more spiritual films will be made showing those of different races, or anyone who is different, getting on together, and showing how to accept others as they are, and how to get along with them. Movies have a tremendous worthwhile effect in developing the frequency of coming together. Viewers watching a film on screen are impacted in a big way when they see the proof of racist behaviour in the story of the movie, and it helps them to understand racial tolerance.

The members of the different cultures and races are prepared to work together to help everyone get along. They will notice the differences between the races and cultures and the ways they are affected by living in the same areas, to discover what they have to do to be on the right track, to bring good results. When confusion is eliminated from the world, the mixed-up interpretations and wrong assumptions made by people about the different races and cultural behaviours will be straightened out.

Here on Earth, we have lessons, and we just naturally have them in our day-to-day living, including in the interactions we have with others, and when we agree or disagree on things openly, we are learning lessons without even realising it. Coming to agreements without realising it leads us forward, and we go ahead with a view to see what happens next. What you agree on is always the right decision to follow, as that is what is meant to happen.

Cultures have celebrations on specific dates by having ceremonies or festivals. These ceremonies are organised exactly, with reliable details of what is to be done by the performers, the location, the date and those who will attend. For example, Chinese New Year celebrations have rituals that they follow, with the exact date of the new year, which is different each year, and with a different animal symbol for each year. There is a total of twelve different animals that follow the same sequence in order for the twelve years and then begin with the first animal again. This celebration uplifts the spirits of those participating and observing, and it is a positive experience that makes them feel part of their culture.

Cultural behaviours are very ingrained in people's way of living. Until they realise that we are all one, each race and culture will continue their behaviours. The core understanding is that races and cultures need to be set free from their ingrained beliefs and behaviours. In society, races and cultural behaviours will transform a little bit further, more and more, with the universe supporting this manifestation. It will flow out to be a full transformation of race and culture where there is no racism. Our future is worldwide unity with just one culture.

People long for, and pray for world peace, but do not know how to bring it about or how to get there. We have to transform the reality. It may take a while because all of the confusion in the world must be eliminated first. To have an awakening we have to come along together in companionship, and this will help to dissolve the confusion. The long-lasting thoughts in people's subconscious mind keep playing over and over in them, from the living of reality in third-dimensional conflict, and it seems that they never get solved. We have to evolve up two dimensions higher, to have the serenity, the new oneness connection and the powerful transformation that we are ready for in our mind's eye and beyond.

As we stream along and learn more, our third eye wakes up more so that we can have better intuition, and more powerful premonitions of the future turning around in a beautiful way. Our old learning, which is our thoughts and our weak perception and the standard way we have been told to live, is no longer relevant and no longer works.

The new beings that are being born in this time will communicate their new thoughts from their intelligence on how to create what we want and need. The recently born children have come to the Earth from the frequency of the new energy of the Age of Aquarius. There will be greater understanding with the fifth dimension, as more ideas can come to mind with its frequencies.

Cultures have a big effect on behaviour. They have to eliminate racism or at least tolerate the different races. All races have to fit into the cultural behaviours of where they are living. So often people are living in countries that have many different cultural behaviours, and in some other countries people are highly likely to have a few different cultures around them.

The independence that races and cultures have from each other means that people who are capable of doing things, particularly when they put their minds to it, will work hard and with integrity to show achievement and to be paid adequately for their work.

As people cooperate more, it enables races and cultures to tolerate each other substantially, and this is necessary for working together for the special purpose that we all want - overall peace. When we work together and collaborate, we reach the love inside us that we sacrificed in the fourth dimension when fear controlled us, and we now give out love to others, as we go into the fifth dimension. It is as though we are already there at the doorstep in the loving perfection of the fifth dimension. From there you just step right into the fifth dimension with trust, living within the center-point of your community, with the races and cultures in each country practicing their uplifting certified arts and ceremonies, according to the rules of that country. People must stay within the boundaries and take each step as it comes for transformation and not go overboard. They must adhere to the rules, keeping together within the same boundaries and staying in the same timeline. If they go over the boundaries they are going too far.

The topic of racism and cultural behaviour has a big effect with its impact on international peace, as it all has to unfold and go forward in the right way.

Globalisation has facilitated cross-cultural collaboration and artistic exchange like never before. Artists from diverse backgrounds gather together, combining their unique perspectives, techniques and cultural influences to create works that transcend borders. Cultures have blended influences from the artists that have worked hard and transcended borders, to connect calmly to work things out the way they should be. Artists use their art-work to portray their culture, and their artistic representation controls the way their cultural identity is perceived.

Cultural ceremonies with national cultural costumes gather people together of the same culture in ceremonial tasks, bringing them together with warmth to get on well and contribute to what has to be done. Recognition of the meanings of cultural things and what is happening in races and cultures will lead to a better life for everyone in their gatherings. Taking part in rituals brings people in that culture together, gathering to cooperate, and supporting each other to do the rituals.

Hard work is the way to get everything done. It is important to feel contentment and have a purpose in your life, so that you are living purposefully, for your wellbeing.

The accomplishment of the races and cultures interacting, with the support of the universe, has the expected outcome of spreading and increasing the one cultural behavioural system that is right for everyone. Cultural development is enjoyable, with the interacting and the enthusiasm of people following instructions that bring ongoing upward movement.

The confusion in the world caused a downward movement to the crossover point of working through the darkest hour of fourth-dimensional reality. Then it turns around for us when an uplift in energy with the fifth dimension unites all cultures as one for our new civilisation.

Referendum results show divisions between races and cultures in the government parties they support. Not all parties support the different cultures. Action needs to be taken to deliver progress on improving cultural behaviours. The roundabout goes around so we have progress in every way, allowing us to work together with flexibility to obtain the outcome we desire. The cultures have a thriving competent ability, along with the important wellbeing, to live and work well doing a good job, with us all throughout the world creating peace together.

The art of conflict goes right back to ancient times, with the races and cultures around the world. However, the art of conflict is in a transition that will lead to transformation, which will eliminate conflict. It takes time for conflicts to transition; however, the support of the universe and the support of information such as in this book, will help to move things along at a much quicker rate. It is very helpful if you have a clear mind and an extremely positive attitude, by looking up as though it is already there. The intuition and envisaging is strong. This is your gut feeling and facts you receive from your intuition, combining with your imagining for a clearer outcome so that what is supposed to happen works out.

As things go on, we will realise everything is connected; we are going to have racial tolerance, and as we come together, we will eliminate racism and unite under one culture.

CHAPTER 12

NATIONALISM AND XENOPHOBIA

Nationalism is a strong loyalty, with enthusiasm or zealousness, to your own country. Xenophobia is the fear or hatred of strangers or foreigners. These are separate things, and we can compare them. Nationalism emphasises pride in your country and the belief that it is superior to others. Power goes together with nationalism, as you want your country to stand out as the most powerful and to win any conflict. There are pros and cons of nationalism. It can give individuals a sense of identity and belonging, a sense of patriotism and unity within a nation. But it can also create divisions among groups because of disagreements about policy, race and conflicts. Nationalism can be taken to extremes. Xenophobia is a negative force; it is a nasty fearfulness. Currently a number of countries have a xenophobic atmosphere, and it is imperative that the consequences of xenophobia are known.

These forces of nationalism and xenophobia will continue in nations until we understand we are all one, and that the consequences of what we do brings it right back to us; what we put out in the energy of our thoughts, words and actions, returns. Unifying and understanding dissolves fear and gains support to come together. Dreariness creates dreadfulness with our thoughts and fears. There is an upsurge worldwide by governments to counteract nationalism and xenophobia, as tears and turmoil continue, and the fear that is behind all of this cannot be let go of.

Understanding xenophobic nationalism is knowing that things have to get worse before they get better, and this puts fear into people's minds, as they think that things are already bad enough in the world. They are very afraid of war and the destruction and trauma that goes with it. But let us stop being fearful and get on the track of being fearless in every way. Things will always work out the way they are supposed to, even if they get far worse beforehand. When people know that what is meant to happen will happen, it helps them to continue with the things they need to do in their daily lives with less distress and more companionship.

Nationalism is not xenophobia but is just as bad. The issues with these two requires organisation to work out how to eliminate xenophobia. We need to know the right way to eradicate xenophobia to gain peace in the nations. The national flag of the country is raised everywhere to show support of their nation, especially at national or community events, and it is a symbol of national pride. At the United Nations they have big discussions and come to agreements over things, and this can ease the tension between nationalistic countries. The debates can cause a lot of friction as nations can get tense or angry, but they have to work in with the other nations in the discussions. The various nations have different interpretations, different emotions and different ways that they do things. Peace talks and ceasefires do not last because there is not enough understanding and knowledge on the part of the human beings. Human theory is that if we keep having conflicts in order for our side to win, then this will end all wars in the world, and we can live in peace. We have to go further than this. The law of cause and effect brings back to you what you put out in the energy of what you think, say and do. Also, the understanding that everything is connected removes any idea of separation. People will understand about the law of cause and effect as it will become more well-known. This will help with the xenophobia situation in all nations and will connect people more.

Governments and leaders need to notice nationalism and xenophobia and have the discipline to deal with it in a sensible way with high standards, understanding the origins of xenophobia and all its consequences. Understanding the core of the situation can lead to a positive outcome, heading towards a much brighter future with integrity that is exciting, with a happier, hopeful outlook. The reasoning is that people need to have a full understanding of details and consequences and of everything coming together.

Your thoughts that you project out is what you are going to get. If you have a strong fear of foreigners then you would want to get away from them, and you will keep away from foreigners until xenophobia is eliminated and discrimination is no longer, as people wake up to the connection. As the old goes out and the new comes in, foreigners will be treated fairly according to the standard way of living within the nation.

Human beings turning to spirituality is like a magical trick happening. It unites the nation as one and destroys xenophobia so we can all live in one spiritual understanding. Going to sacred spiritual sites, which have strong spiritual energy, and making a wish, puts it into your consciousness so that you will receive the ability in your consciousness to know what is right and wrong in the nation. The natural energy at the sacred sites develops your intuition, as you have to realise what is right and wrong to work together.

After we reach the turning point for fifth-dimensional energy, which will be miraculous to live by here on the Earth plane, every bit of progress that each one of us makes in our day-to-day lives will be supported. Many different races and cultures are forming strategies so that foreigners can move into other nations and interact with other people, as well as be given support without any concerns of xenophobia. As fifth-dimensional energy increases it will displace all discrimination and xenophobia towards foreigners who move into other nations. Nationalism and xenophobia are two different topics but can have the same effects. Governments will make new laws to safeguard foreigners, who have to deal with the authorities to fit in with their nation and their way of behaving so that they can stay there.

Momentum is happening to get through the darkest hour before the dawn, (a well-known proverb that people apply to the situation here on Earth), so we can all unite under one nation. We will trade the nasty fear for loving kindness, as human actions, with universal support, enable an even stronger connection to the universal essence within the one connection. Looking further at national identities, nationalism will blend in with xenophobia, and ways to treat it and deal with it will be figured out. With xenophobia, race has the biggest effect. Foreigners moving into other countries cause upheaval with their beliefs and sexist attitudes, and this in turn creates xenophobia against them and intolerance of their behaviours. They bring their attitudes of oppression and control of women, and they treat the women who were already living in that country in a sexist way, creating resentment and objection from those women who are used to freedom and respect.

The spreading of conflicts and war is unifying us, and conflicts are getting worse. A lot of things have improved for the better in recent decades, but some things have got worse, and these are what people focus on. All the things that have actually got better have been portrayed as being worse by the negative news media, which describes the most negative way of seeing those things, showing positive things as negative.

There are some positive aspects about fear. It makes you aware of danger. If you didn't feel fear, you would not know how dangerous some things can be, for example fire, which can burn or kill you. When you go to a beach and see a 'no swimming' sign because of a dangerous current or sharks, this causes fear, and you would likely choose not to go swimming.

A universal year one is the most powerful year to begin something new. To stabilise relationships with foreigners and nations, it is best to work with the universe and start in a universal year one and this will help to create control with the power of stabilisation. The year 2026 will be a universal year one. 2+0+2+6=10. Reducing to a single digit: 1+0=1.

The aspects of fear in the material world have advantages and disadvantages. As we move ahead with nationalism and xenophobia, knowing it is combined with the other topics we have touched upon in these chapters, many of the fears will decrease, as we are moving further into the fifth dimension. We will live by the universe's rules and come to know that fear is no longer needed, and that the causes of the fear are gone. The elements of fear on Earth may no longer exist, or if they do they will not come near you, or you will not be affected in any way as you will understand the fifth-dimensional world. The causes of fear are within ourselves, from the third and fourth dimensions of the material world.

A new outcome is created with everything we do, and the universe supports us. Looking again at xenophobia on its own, it is important to address it as it can have dangerous effects in society, because of people's prejudice against anyone who is different to themselves. Learning how to cope with xenophobia towards you can be difficult and people do not know what to do about it. They can ask friends and family for help, go to counselling for guidance, or go to a doctor for a medical prescription.

I know we are heading towards a better world, and you do too from reading this book. It will be worthwhile to get that inner peace. The contract agreement from the universe is for world peace, and as we support each other with friendliness and kindness, the universe does its automatic work of supporting us.

Citizen's fears and phobias are recognised by high up people in society, whereby strong leaders and highly capable democracies are already trying to gather together, to work out the situation regarding world peace and what to do about it. The governments and authorities agree on the development sequence required to have world peace, and I have written about what to do and how to move on, from my own intuition.

Everything that exists on Earth is connected, and everything that is happening proves that we are all connected. This connection, along with the integration of what is needed, automatically supports everyone onto a better financial basis, so that everyone receives an equal share and no one will live in the dust or be badly mistreated. Receiving a fair go is when it is fair and square, and when there is a compassionate connection to all human beings that you truly admire, with peace and justice. It takes work to obtain that attitude of justice and the attitude of what is needed to have health and wellbeing, accepting everyone as they are and having a healthy lifestyle.

Fifth-dimensional frequency and its controlled development of support, (the universe supporting us), will unite us as one and bring out our courageous laughter that we thought we would never be able to do. Now it has happened, and we look back in astonishment at the past and how badly we treated others.

As our destiny of unity arrives, the United Nations becomes much stronger as it will work to unify us with agreements, since it will be possible to understand one another, and the old, ingrained beliefs will fade away, being no longer needed. As an estimate, over the next several years we will see the transformation to unity with the extreme help of the universe. Transformation and change are two distinct things that stand out. Change is modifying day-to-day actions, while transformation involves modifying core beliefs and long-term behaviours in profound ways.

We are moving forward to the goal of global unification. Businesses and governments will also have change and transformation. The change of our actions and beliefs supports us on to unity for global peace. With unity we will do away with our fears, including nationalism and xenophobia and the fear of foreigners.

CHAPTER 13

WAR, PEACE AND JUSTICE

To understand the relationship between these three things, I have put them together in this chapter to explain how war and peace can result in justice.

War is fighting, often caused by hatred between countries, that is ongoing and bitter and does not get resolved. War is generally revengeful as the attacker wants to pay someone back for what they have done, and it can often escalate from conflicts. It is a very damaging process that harms innocent citizens. The controversy continues on, as the two sides cannot agree, therefore their opposing demands are not met, and no one wins.

Peace is happiness with playing, fun and friendliness. Joy and harmony from playing makes life much more enjoyable. We will look at the example of play-fights. These often occur between children, gently attacking each other, such as punching and friendly wrestling. Parents may also have play-fights with their children. I know I have enjoyed the company of playful children over the years when I was young and enjoying the laughter and fun. By combining the two words play and fight as one, we can see there is a positive arrangement (or sequence) as they are two separate words that can neutralise each other when formed into one word.

Let us look at 'Tug of War' now.

This is a game with two teams and a thick rope, with one team holding one end of the rope and the other team holding the opposite end of the rope. There is a coach who marks the center of the rope as well as marking a center point on the ground. Some words are shouted, such as "on your marks, get set, heave" or perhaps a number countdown "3, 2, 1, heave." Both teams on each end tug the rope as hard as they can in a competition to pull the other team towards them over the line in the center. Once this has happened, the coach raises their hand and shouts "this team are the winners". There is a lot of excitement and controversy sometimes if the players think the coach is not being fair.

Thriving on competition is a big thing for some members of society who have a competitive nature. The winners are excited and celebrate with drinks, a medal or trophy if it is a competition with team finals. That is the way of exciting team competitions. Let us now look at another version of the Tug of War game.

'Tug of Peace.'

This game rallies the participants to cooperate and unite. Let us look further into this and study it more. You still have the organisation needed, the coach, the rope and two different teams. The game begins the same with the coach centering the rope at the center point on the ground. There may still be the same starting signals given and countdown to tell the teams to start their play. The big difference is, that when the coach says the word "heave", the teams cooperate and work together. They pull the rope backwards and forwards over the line in the center, as they connect with each other in the 'Tug of Peace'. This behaviour is better mannered. Let me explain how the teamwork can be deeper with the 'Tug of Peace'. When the teams receive the signal to "heave", not only do both teams tug the rope backwards and forwards over the line in the center, but they actually share the rope by letting it go past both finish lines on either side. This is balanced peaceful excitement, as they have developed a new way of thinking and understanding, new awareness and a new way of uniting.

We will understand the play in ourselves that is supported by the universe. There will be a large, magnificent domino effect that takes place, whereby the 'Tug of Peace' is an example of the attitudes and behaviour of 'share and play' that is needed to have worldwide peace.

Wars are often associated with dictatorships that have total power in their countries, where the dictator behaves badly and is a strong, selfish, revengeful narcissist who does not care about others. Strong narcissists do not change; they will always enjoy hurting others and taking revenge. The mental health disorder of narcissism needs to be treated, but there is no cure, although counselling or talk therapy may help in some cases to moderate or control this disorder that is harmful to others.

When the strong leaders make ceasefire agreements, this is an arrangement to create peace between certain countries, between certain calendar dates, to try to stabilise the situation so that there is a chance of peace. Ceasefire agreements can be good when they bring the parties together to negotiate, to help contain the conflict, with the purpose of fulfilling the world's destiny to be at peace.

New cells in the membrane surrounding the human brain are connecting up from the thoughts in the conscious and subconscious mind so that the entire brain has a permanent new sense of logical understanding. It is important to let go of old baggage to be able to move ahead in your life. The baggage is garbage, so throw it out of your system. This can be hard to do but is necessary. Guided meditations, yoga or tai chi can be very beneficial. Going to a counsellor or therapist can be very emotional but talking about your issues can help. They may also give you a guided meditation so you can work on your negative emotions and thoughts to transform them. All your emotions are programmed into your mind, and your cells are connected up, so transforming your negative emotions can lead to them becoming positive.

Theoretically things always work out for the better, and the reality shows that things do get partly better in individual lives. More teamwork is needed by all of us interacting together in oneness for world peace. All people together are excited about the good things happening and they are accessing the universe's 100% support. The universe gives us accuracy to that degree.

The ongoing wars and battles that seem never ending, and the development and production of nuclear missiles, along with their testing to ensure that they work well and are powerfully destructive, are happening now. As the nuclear testing and production increases by powerful governments who want the power to threaten other countries, it makes the ordinary citizens worry about the safety and future of the world. All of the countries that have nuclear weapons are causing fear and worry in other countries and their populations, because of the known impact if those weapons were to be used in a conflict or war to attack. The populations of the countries that have nuclear weapons are also fearful of them being used to attack because they know there would be retaliation strikes back on their country.

They know their government would attack others to defend their country if necessary.

Some people are fearful that doomsday will happen, but it never does and never will, as things have to go on and on, so people can keep living and learning all the lessons they need. World war three may happen and will have to happen, if people do not realise the damage done on Earth with the physical and spiritual sides being out of balance. All of the wars and conflicts that humans have already caused, and all of the disasters, have not brought people together enough. If humans do not get their act together it will be time for World War III to break out. The spiritual world needs to be proven before we will all work together to heal the negative karma, that has been man-made for thousands of years. World War III would be a nuclear war with a lot of destruction and harm from radiation, and fear that doomsday is near. It is natural to feel that doomsday is arriving when the situation gets so hateful. Every day a new dawn arises, as that always has to happen. Conflicts and wars will keep happening until humans learn the lessons and no longer want revenge.

Pray for peace but prepare for war, is the attitude of some, who hope that other countries will not start conflicts or war, but instead will respect their land boundaries, live peacefully and respect each other.

Let us look at war, peace and justice together and explore them. War is killing, power and revenge. Peace, on the other hand, is forgiveness and living in a calm state. Justice is about fairness, equality and taking right action. War is raw and does a lot of harm, not only to those who are fighting, but also to all the innocent people caught up in it. To finally have justice, we need to be reminded about oneness. Also, we need to remember all the different topics discussed in this book, to have no doubt that we are coming together. The more the pieces connect into the puzzle, as described in Chapter 1, the more it builds up justice and fairness in human society and gathers momentum towards the peace we all want, with oneness.

Even though the universe is connected 100%, it can be more powerful with its support depending on what universal year we are in. How long will wars last? Ongoing wars are terrible, and people grow weary of the destruction both in their country and in their lives. The length of time the war lasts can depend on the universal year. Wars are always strong and long lasting here on Earth when they begin in a universal one year, as it is a beginning year, which makes it very powerful with acceleration from the universe. Universal calendar dates have meaning and power also, when the date is added to make a total.

For example, the year 2025. Adding the numbers 2+0+2+5=9. So, 2025 is a universal nine year, which is an ending year, so hopefully some wars may end this year. The universal years are in nine-year cycles, from years one to nine, and 2026 will be a universal one year, which is a year of new beginnings. This is the study of numerology. If we know the numerology system, it can help us understand the universal energy of each year and what the energy is supporting. If we begin our unity in a one year (2026) or a master number eleven year (2027), we will be able to encompass far greater closeness of humanity, whereby the citizenry may create peace amongst people with understanding, without any trouble. The calculation of the universal year, and the support it gives us in what we need to do, still supports us even if we are not consciously aware of it in our lives and activities.

Our new knowledge is opening us up to what it is about, with new rules, to allow peace and unity. The government will put in place new grounded rules for unity and for peace. Universal laws will be more widely known. The development of world peace is like a secret, as there seems no chance of it happening on Earth today. For readers of this book, all the obstacles written about in these chapters will make them realise we can unify.

The loving light of the lightworkers, and their commitment on Earth, will lift the vibration within the lightworkers themselves, and we will notice the enjoyment of the raised frequency without knowing the cause. People will realise, learn, and be informed by hearing about things and feeling the higher energy. Teams of lightworkers are working together to pray and send love and healing out to the Earth and its people. News teams and networks will change their attitudes and will air positive news, and this, along with the love of the lightworker teams, helps transform the energy to have the best possible outcome.

The Earth is holding on to negative energy, as there is so much of it, and we are actually subconsciously aware of this negative energy in the Earth's atmosphere, even though we are in a higher era now (the fourth dimension). It is trapped in the atmosphere, and the Earth cannot get rid of it because of the confusion from wars etc. amongst humans. The Earth is grasping the negative energy tightly, so it does not cause too much destruction, as this negative energy is the reason why so many natural disasters happen, and is the cause of so much confusion, because it is the darkest hour. If it wasn't for the lightworkers, and also the natural disasters that partly release and reduce the negative energy, along with the help of extraterrestrials, and angels from the angelic realm, the Earth would have exploded by now. It would not be able to cope with such an overdose of negative energy.

At the present time we are living in there is still war, but these wars will not last because of the power of the lightworkers, and the universe's support. We may say that war will soon be a thing of the past, and with the support of the information in this book, everyone will have peace residing within them. As a result of that, we will see, on a much larger scale, peace outside ourselves. This will go on to world peace, as our collective consciousness knows, from its awareness of what we see.

In time to come we will make better use of our days, and we will have more relaxation and recreation time, as it is important to be stress-free.

We have to do our transformation within ourselves with the perspective of a new understanding; it means we are improving ourselves. What is coded within us is the genetic codes that are part of our essence. These will cause the transformation from within us and outside of us that we have to do. The coding system within our DNA has all the cells that are telling our mind what to do, then our mind tells US. Then we have to prepare and organise what to do to get to the outcome of worldwide peace.

People are seeking the truth about what has been hidden in the dark for centuries by those who had the control and the power to keep it secret. In the short term we need to have trust in the process of coming together, so we can prepare for the long-range future of connecting as one, in unity, as has been predicted by us.

We need to become more casual with the new world in order to adjust to it and fit in with it, and as we come together to do that, the universe will automatically support us better and substantially, with equality. The new age practice becomes formal as people work in and adjust to it.

Governments need the support of other governments as they try to solve financial crises, war, homelessness, poverty and low-income issues. In time to come, governments can be more supportive to each other, communicate more, and help each other out on a financial basis.

Along with the new age, the veil on the spiritual side is being loosened and done away with so we can understand how to cure all the suffering and how to stop the wars. Our behaviour will begin to change as we go through the new age process. We will have strong communication that will go well, with its superb agenda, and a lot can be decided without any breakdowns in the proceedings.

When we interact with one another we learn skills from the leaders to understand about the right and wrong treatment of other people. We will come to have a clear sense of what is right and wrong so we can have calmness and mental stability. We need to know what is right to have peace, and we need to know what is wrong that causes war. War does not get us anywhere. Knowing what constitutes the right and wrong treatment of others provides a fundamental central basis for obtaining world peace. We need justice, as we need set rules that are applied. There will be a justice system put in place by governments worldwide to make rules to support peace.

There will be more cooperation from governments to send food to warzone countries, where people are crying out in poverty. The innocent civilians caught up in wars need as much support, kindness and caring as possible. In the warlike areas, fighting is often very bitter and on a large scale. When we come to a clear sense of right and wrong, ceasefire agreements will be put into effect for a longer amount of time. Change can be made on a big scale to get the outcome you want, by uniting in cooperation.

The desire for peace gets stronger, the longer that wars last on Earth. Ceasefires need to continue longer, but it seems stupid when they do not last. We have to learn cooperation so that ceasefires are lasting, and so that all human beings can be at peace.

War and peace are seen as opposites, but when we cooperate, it brings them together so we can find solutions. If we all realise war is not getting us anywhere, then our new education will teach us to share and will bring us together in unity. We will see true justice in the power of completing the warlike domination of Pisces and entering the loving peace of Aquarius which will bring harmony.

Universal energy supports our lives and what we choose to do, so that in the Age of Pisces it supported the wars. In the new Age of Aquarius, it supports us with more awareness of our connection and confronts us with the necessity to find peace within ourselves, so that we can all connect in peace to work with everyone else. It may sound a bit far-fetched that we will be much more loving to each other. There are so many different types of people in this world, all with their own ways of thinking and doing things. The pull of world peace is strong, as so many people want it, although it seems that there is no way of getting it.

Until people understand that we are all connected, and we are all one, there will always be ongoing conflict. We have to work through the confusion and understand that we have to look deeply into spirituality and dig out the facts of what it is all about. Knowledge will be organised outside of the material world for us to know, and we will be able to prove the afterlife. We will all be able to work together, all over the world, with calmness and mental stability giving us the focus and stamina to live in peace and harmony interactively with others.

The more we are in alignment with Aquarius, the more good works governments do to better things. They do this consciously from the new frequency of the universe, but do not even notice the new frequency of Aquarius as they are not open to that information. The governments must pinpoint exactly what they want in their agreements, but they still will have to compromise. Both sides will get what they want but will have to meet halfway in-between. They will find that the agreements they compromised on, turn out a lot better than what they thought they would.

When governments change their ways of thinking, it will have a big impact on us as it will change our thinking so that we will know exactly what is right and wrong. We will understand that there is no longer any need for competition and will realise the connection gained through cooperation.

We are not SEPARATE. We are ALL CONNECTED and all in it together, meaning we are all ONE. People will understand the connection of things, and we will achieve a high standard of working together to do what is needed to be done. The energy of the universe is powerful. Once you know the information such as contained in this book, you will know the steps to take.

We have been unable to achieve the goal of world peace that we have been longing for, as we did not know how to go about it, and did not even know what the first step would be, as the information was not provided.

A ping-pong effect takes place when the public reads information such as in this book, and they comprehend it, and with their understanding they follow the steps to take action, leading to the biggest effect that has ever taken place here on Earth.

CHAPTER 14

DEFEAT VICTORY

Some people love the feeling of winning and having victory as they have a competitive mindset. They have to win, whether it is a sport, a game or a war, they have to win over the other side, team, person or country. They are obsessed with winning; it is ingrained in them to win and come in first place, and they cannot give up this attitude.

Let us look at the advantages there are when people cooperate instead of competing. You can agree on things, and this makes games more enjoyable. You will have connections with others through cooperation, rather than competition.

Cooperation is a way of aligning people with caring and sharing. It is difficult for people to see the connection between competition and cooperation, because they like to receive the first prize or the medal. In time to come there will not be any competition, just friendly games, and if people still want to score, it will be in a cooperative spirit. There will be a conversion between the two sides, with there being no more competition as it will turn into cooperation.

There will be opposition to those who want to end competition and replace it with cooperation, by those who enjoy competition and winning. Victory is separate and cooperation is connected. We need to defeat victory to move away from separation and become connected.

Government leaders will give messages about what is needed to be done to effect the changeover to cooperation and connection. Eventually this will become law. It will be a step-by-step development process to go through the change in thinking to that of cooperation. People will follow on themselves with their own thinking and their own working out of the next steps. The steps will work effectively to soften the ingrained attitudes, and once they are softened they can be eased out. Both governments and citizens must make the effort to work for cooperation. Rules must be made so people cannot return to competition but must keep going with cooperation. Focusing on cooperation will result in the phasing out of competitive attitudes.

The victory way is where winning is ingrained in your mindset to be a sports champion and defeat your opponents to receive the highest medal at the big final ceremony; congratulations are given on the achievement of winning over others. Dismantling this way of thinking will make a new start. It may seem too difficult. It has to be remarkably well done for people to support it, and it will be a prolonged lengthy process that seems never-ending. But being fair to everyone is important. The programming about the pursuit of victory has to be changed so that athletes do not crave to be the best, either locally or in the world.

From my writing that comes from my own true self, I know we need to find the self-reliance in everyone and amongst everyone to have full cooperation over victory. All will agree to combine to release the need to have victory over others, the need to feel superior to others or better than others because you have won over them.

We have to know the right methods to defeat victory. What is actually needed to do this? When we are at the crossroads between competition and cooperation, there are arguments about what is best to do, with many taking standpoints on the issues. In a time of collaboration, the defeat of victory will be applauded. Arguing will be caused by people's doubts about changing. Many do not want to change and do not want to even talk about it. They have to acknowledge the advantages of cooperation to be able to even begin to change. It has to be guaranteed at the crossroads that we are going to be moving ahead into cooperation and uniting in this, with enforcement by government and community leaders. People will instinctively know the truth inside themselves about what is best, and this enhances the uniting. If you stick to what you know is right and the action you want to take, it will all work out for you at the crossroads of fourth-dimensional reality that we are in now. You must push to put in place what you know is right and what you are capable of.

As they go through the crossroads, everyone will feel they are in the right place in their minds and thoughts, and they will be in their comfort zone. If they want competition and victory during the crossroads time, they will have it. If they want cooperation during that time, they will have it.

After the crossroads time, the unfolding of laws from government and community leaders will result in thorough progress with cooperation. Those listening to the leaders will perceive the meaning and outcome of their words and will form their view of what is right for themselves. In my writing, I am describing and identifying what is involved in cooperation and bringing all people to agree, to adjust current reality.

The government will make laws that ban victory. The public will be in sync with the government and will see the effects of the laws. It will not cause upheaval, debate or controversy as the public will be adjusting and working their way into cooperation. Eventually everyone will come to see what is right in the new age, as there will be cooperation and understanding amongst everybody.

Leaders will teach development skills to the citizens, so they can learn how to change their thinking and develop cooperation, and then they can work well with others. Humans take pleasure in victory and thrive on it. They cannot let go. This lasts until eventually it will get lost amongst all the new ideas of unity, as the domino effect takes place. Caring to share is a much better way of adjusting to world peace because of its unifying effect.

From everything I have said in this chapter, is there sufficient data to implement the changeover from victory to cooperation?

Yes, there is!

Some of you still may not agree, but you will see the outcome and results of all those doing a good job, supposedly within fifth-dimensional reality. To be in fifth dimension the cooperation has to be fair. The layout of cooperation for coming together is mainly set in place by the communities with the support of the government, who have contact with, and help from the extraterrestrials, and also having proof of the afterlife for a new age. World problems will be identified, and the exact ways to deal with them. The proof of heaven will enable the flow of the solutions that will be implemented.

Eventually the word 'victory' will no longer be used in our vocabulary as it will not be relevant. It will fade out and will ultimately be wiped out when the new age comes in.

A general order will be made by the government for everyone to cooperate and work together without competition. Depending on how well that order works out, the government will make more orders, and this process will continue.

With all the other obstacles (to world peace) from the other chapters in this book also changing at the same time that victory is changing, it means people's attitudes will be changing on all of these matters at the same time, and this will help to change the victory attitude. As we will be getting to know the universal laws, especially the law of oneness, this will help as well, as we will be seeing new ways of looking at things that have been prevalent on Earth for a very long time.

The words 'DEFEAT VICTORY' speak for themselves. They are bold words, and those two words put together identify what we want to focus on and achieve. People will know and understand what the two words mean, and they also see how they can change into cooperation. It may seem unbelievable, but if we can imagine it and focus on it we can create the improbable, as not only are we coming together and cooperating, but we also see the fading away as the two words turn things around into cooperation. As these two words automatically flow and take over the focus, everyone comes into full wonderful cooperation, and then the victory word evaporates (in the future) when it becomes irrelevant.

Cooperating defeats victory. Readers may understand that being preoccupied with victory, as I have written, goes on to be defeated. Getting rid of the competition and thereby defeating victory helps increase inner peace. Personally I (the author) have found a new way of coping with victory, by undermining it through speaking out about its disadvantages and negative effects, whilst at the same time praising the benefits of cooperation. The challenge in all of this is to find 'love' in the word 'defeat'. There are negative associations connected to the word 'defeat', as it means losing. The word 'love' is the right word to defeat victory. Love has a pure essence that defeats it and brings cooperation amongst everybody.

The outcome of cooperation is that it will bring everyone together to work well with each other. Firstly, this defeats all wars and conflicts. Secondly, there will be cooperation and achievement in playing sports better. The leaders of the community will develop a daily program with rules and instructions about how sports are to be played without victory, with fairness to all. Once cooperation is fully in place the situation is calmed down, which is victory being defeated wisely.

New information on how to go about having world peace, such as written in this book, will be heard and noticed by citizens who want to change things and who will strongly persuade their governments to do something. The more progress we make with eliminating victory, and the more that cooperation takes over, the more we will feel inspired within ourselves. All the cooperation amongst ourselves will change things, with everything coming together and unifying, which is essential for world peace. When the leaders in power gather in unity with the locals to be involved in community-type work, this creates a domino effect, as the locals all want to be involved when the leaders are there. The locals will provide support by having 'working bees'. Universal support will also work with us to receive gains. The locals have to be given the right information to do what needs to be done.

They will be doing the same community work that will be rostered in a fair way.

It is important to have inner peace. Cooperating and working together results in a lot of inner peace because of the feeling of comfort. Getting things right for inner peace must come first before world peace arrives.

The voice over the meadows from the mountaintops has called for cooperation by people in everything and in every way. Truly-minded communities are listening more and coming into cooperation from what they are hearing. They cannot understand exactly what the message is, so they are on standby, and full cooperation cannot be put into place.

Believing in a new outcome that actually reverses the old stuff and moves us ahead into another age that is spiritually evolved will inspire peace everywhere, in you, and in the world. The ongoing agreement to defeat the maintaining of the structured competition is always highly charged, with we ourselves being leaders regarding what we KNOW; we KNOW to DEFEAT the competition. We can defeat victory with politeness between people, and the domino effect allows US to become even stronger leaders to defeat the opposition with courtesy that is inspiring to us. We have been given the privilege of defeating victory from what we have learnt from higher community leaders who have taught us, the citizens, so well.

What is IN us has to be programmed into our consciousness and then go through to be programmed into our subconscious, and to be that ingrained that we have the knowing of what to do to transform competition into cooperation. The achievement of defeating victory can be likened to burning down a tall tower in outrage, as humans are so tired of revenge that has never solved anything.

All of the news coverage is fully international, spreading the new message around the world for all to hear, so that the world's citizens in different continents feel more connection to their fellow humans in other parts of the world. We are realising that our behaviour has to be reliable to defeat victory internationally. Our sixth sense is working well in an extreme state of cooperation together with everyone worldwide to dissolve all confusion. We are weary of confusion, and being at the crossroads point means it is now the darkest hour, but extreme cooperation will completely dissolve it all away. Until confusion is ended, there will still be ongoing war. With confusion nothing seems to get resolved, and there is war, conflict and more revenge that is never-ending. That is why we must come to the realisation that we have to take a cooperative stance in order to work together successfully and to have forgiveness for all the harm done. Until the endless cycle of revenge between enemies is turned into forgiveness, we will keep having the continuous suffering of war in our everyday lives and news. Many of us do not want this, therefore we will be thankful for the new pathway onward, exploiting the growing momentum, to reach the biggest outcome ever, of cooperation.

All the communities and people need to know the force and knowledge of the universe; they need to know what it is about, and they need to know it is connected. They will come to terms with the new teachings of the community at each service or meeting they go to. There has to be interests for people in their communities, that they can gather for, and work together on, to encounter what is new that will get them through to the golden age. The leaders will have to perform well to the citizens at the service meetings. It is essential that they are good leaders. Citizens will demand from their leaders the best proposals for the right policies and solutions. This will leave people with a nice heartfelt feeling of belonging. That nice feeling of belonging inside us is the base of ourselves, and the base of what goes out to create the center of attention of world peace. The center of attention is what is inside all of us, a sense of belonging and feeling secure – the core of everyone working together to do what is right for world peace.

Governments know things that we do not know, that are beyond our belief, and they incorporate things with extraterrestrials. The governments will prove spirituality one day, through scientists, who will be able to obtain information similar to that in this book. This proof will be put onto computers so that people can see it, and it will be used to make laws. Our physical world laws will be replaced with universal laws in the future.

The comparison of the words 'defeat victory', which sound like opposites, shows that defeat means fighting and victory means winning. But when you put the two words together, defeating victory works into cooperation. Taken separately the words are opposites, but when put together the meaning is that victory is defeated and is replaced by coordinated cooperation. We have to see the opposite meanings in the words to see how they go together. The defeating process is a bit frightening; people are questioning it, and there are very ingrained attitudes. It is the darkest hour before the dawn and there is a bit of confusion in the organisation of defeating it. The steps to be taken must be organised to be able to recognise what the outcome will be, and what the benefits of cooperation are, so that both sides will be pleased with the progress toward the outcome and will take pleasure in carrying it out. This defeats the fighting within victory.

The wealth of good things that people saw in victory now have a new meaning and are understood in a new light, with a new outcome, of people gathering in an alliance. The support of both the government and the citizens automatically creates justice. With the universe's support, as the universe has a connection with us, we have everything within us to keep moving forward. All the realisation of our cooperation has become deeply ingrained. This will defeat fear easily and allow peace to bring world unity.

News coverage will be respectful about the physical world and the spiritual world when reporting on aspects of life. This is always supported by the universal order – frequency, awareness, and alignment of our wellbeing. You feel thankful when you think about the new order, with the realigning of energy to have exact alignment with the new age. We are receiving the enhancement to keep up with the new age: following the flow of the movement (to the new age), teaching the leaders, and the speeding up of linear time. From your position of cooperation, you can see what an astonishing achievement has been made.

Part of our own individual essence is also part of the worldwide essence, so that we can all work together collectively for world peace. Our individual essence in ourselves is essential in what we do to reach our goal of peace.

Our intuition knows how to defeat the negative effects of competitive victory wisely and collectively for universal wellbeing, as well as our own. As we all move on together, we can become more organised and more connected with the support of universal consciousness, the universal energy that fully supports us with its 100% connection. We are sussing out how to quickly and skilfully coordinate all the information we have gathered, using our gut intuition and perceptions to enhance our teamwork even more strongly. We actually create a strong domino effect ourselves with our actions, by working together, along with the universe's support, as it is connected with us. The domino effect can produce the fastest and largest results of what we desire, and we can have some definite fun with this.

It is hard for us to know that we are connected to all other people, so we have to go step-by-step towards understanding it. The key principle is to teach and learn this process in steps as human beings.

The main aim of defeating victory is the education process of knowing everything is all oneness. The powerful cooperation is defeating what is competitive, even if in a playful way.

CHAPTER 15

TIME AND MATTER

Time and matter are connected in an astounding way. Time is an illusion, and matter is everything around us that exists. Time has formed from matter, from the rotation of the Earth and the duration and length of days and nights, and the orbiting of the Earth around the Sun. We use clocks and watches for timekeeping. It is really the Sun that we tell the time with, from the Earth's rotation on a daily basis. The planets in our solar system have powerful meanings that will assist us all to transcend to a new level with their cycle around the Sun that supports us on to the Age of Aquarius here in the material world. It is so forceful as the universe is connected, and as the planets in our solar system have their alignment, it forces and pushes Aquarius into the material world. Our decision making will be done with the precision of a mental state that is in the frequency of a new order of awareness. With the world order we need to understand all matters to get things right for working collectively, and do away with phobias, discrimination and other issues that prevent this. With the compilation of matter, that is everything formed from the alignment of our wellbeing, it stays on track to support the highest attainment of working connectedly to support our destiny of peace.

The new generation coming in will turn and transform things from what they know, as their frequency is much more spiritually organised due to their awareness of the purpose they are here for, to bring us into the fifth dimension and set us free, to be super beneficial in the higher dimension.

Time and matter both work with numbers. Western astrology is interesting in that all of us are born at a precise time, and an astrology chart can be made of the astrological influences on us at our exact time of birth. Not everyone is aware of astrology or is interested in getting their birth chart, or they may not agree with it. The chart shows your life path and personality traits. Your astrology at birth and the position of the planets is a factor in your life and destiny.

We learn and develop new skills in our daily lives with the attributes that we have. Interactions take place between many people about knowledge and drama, in different areas at the same time, and it is not noticed, and this is holding us back from progress. There are positive or negative consequences, but the location where it happens does not record it therefore it has to happen again and again until we learn from it. We do not understand and mistrust the information as we do not know if it is just in our imagination. The universe always supports us with its energy no matter what our behaviour is like, and the power of its supportive energy relates to the universal year number it is, in numerology, on the Earth plane. To expand on this, we are coming towards a stronger golden age than the last one in Atlantis as more planets are aligned. There could be other opinions from this, but this is strongly what I feel from my own intuition.

The stream of alignment is flowing with hiccups and coughs from all the old baggage and confusion throwing itself out. With the alignment of the planets in our solar system we have been moving up further dimensionally, from the interpretation of the new information that we have been given. Faith will keep us on the right track to achieve our goal. Our track is leading us to the new world, moving us on our journey using the information that we know about the track we are on. We will know what we need and our thoughts will support us with the universe, to have what we need.

The energy of matter can be used with understanding to obtain a professional outcome just by focusing on a single thought and noticing how powerful that is and then repeating it and standardising it. The cells that connect up in our own mind are in sequence with the membranes around the brain so it can do its duty of creating our reality. Programmed transformation is in connection within the substance of matter, with all the numbers, to transform the material side and spiritual side. The capacity to participate in spirituality is increasing, with psychics being more accepted to make predictions about what will be organised to create a better future, and people will listen to them.

People have been developing their own ways of thinking, and in the second half of the twentieth century there was some alignment of the planets that shifted the consciousness of people's thoughts for them to gain more insight and develop fresh thinking. Some people work hard and do not get rewarded for it, and bad things happen to very good people, which seems unfair. This makes people question why it is that they have to suffer great difficulties while others have it easy with no trouble at all. This is a new understanding of contemporary thoughts, seeing the fluctuating progress from the contemporary moments, that make you think about things in different ways from the misunderstanding that you have been taught from the Christian Bible. It makes people rethink about Bible verses that do not match up or make sense, or fit in with the struggle of daily life, and what you do on a day-to-day basis, living your life in an ongoing process. Some of the Bible writings are good, and beneficial to you in your daily life, but others do not make sense or relate to your life. Certain Bible chapters and verses you keep referring to do fit for you in your life; however, others do not. It is confusing when the Bible words you are referring to do not fit into place in your life as you would like them to. This pulls people out of religion, to develop their own spiritual way of thinking that makes more common sense in their daily lives.

If all the information about matter is assembled in alphabetical order it makes it easier to follow and understand where we are at and how to proceed. Matter refers to objects and substances, and also time. We have a oneness connection with all matter that exists. Once heaven is proved, people will have a full understanding of matter. Everything is one with matter, which gives a new perception that begins to unify opposite ideas to get the outcome that brings about world peace, with everyone coming to the same way of thinking.

Time and matter can have a full connection in even more detail. We are all that is; the fact is that we are connected as one to everything there is. This gives us a far more uplifting connection to the spiritual realm and to the essence that provides the support for world peace. When there is proof of heaven, the universal frequency will be much higher. The universe covers the support we need, and as the Age of Pisces comes to its completion, we understand that the veil between both sides is breaking, and we are becoming enlightened with the knowledge that we do not die. We understand that life is everlasting;

our physical body stops serving its purpose, but our spirit lives on for eternity, and even if we choose not to incarnate again because we think we have learned all of life's lessons, our spirit is eternal in the spiritual realm.

When we incarnate here on Earth, we shut off to our subconscious mind where all our past lives we have lived are stored, and we just focus on what we are doing on Earth. It is just as well we cannot remember our past lives as it would disrupt our current incarnation here on Earth, and we would not have the ability to fulfil the essence of our destiny while living in this incarnation.

Everyday facts are the content throughout our consciousness, while allowing for spiritual seeking in the spiritual realm, which is always there for us, even when we dwell on things about it. The conscious is always aware and thinking about things that are happening naturally in our daily lives. We can put our conscious and subconscious minds together purposefully to interact with ourselves to discover the answer to a request. We can do this in our daily life just by being aware that our brain is always interacting fully with both sides of the mind. Can we learn and understand more about it? Not only are there the conscious and subconscious parts of the brain, but the right side of the brain controls the left side of the body, and the left side of the brain controls the right side of our body. Our conscious mind controls all our current awareness, encompassing thoughts, feelings and decision making. In the present moment you are acting from your feelings and making decisions from your thoughts. Our subconscious mind has long-term awareness and ingrained thoughts that are stable and hard to let go of. You can meditate to seek the answers you need regarding your current actions in the present. Being present is not just about connection but also about using your sixth sense and developing your skills to do this correctly. By using your third eye and strong intuition, you can interpret correctly. The stronger your feelings are about your intuition, the more likely it will happen, and sooner.

When you notice that time is just an illusion, you may notice that the stability of the energy changes to a much higher degree. The energy coming in will be much more forceful, showing for a fact that there is only one present. It puts enormous force into place when there is only one present, and as everything is happening at once, we can see everything that is there. Although everything is happening at once, because time is an illusion, here in our material world we are experiencing one thing happening at a time. If you do not wear a wristwatch, then you are not continually looking at the time and worrying about it, and this keeps you in the present. Time is just the calculation (by scientists from the rotation of the Earth) with illusion from matter, and we can do what we like with it in our thoughts.

We have spirit guides to guide us and keep us on track along our life path. We also have guardian angels that we can ask for help, and they ensure that we do not die prematurely before we have planned to. Our guides are always present and available to talk to in our thoughts or aloud, even if we are not aware of them being there. Guides keep us on track for moving ahead to where we are meant to be going, and they will always do the job and be aware of your safety, unless you are supposed to be involved in a crisis. Spirit guides and angels must always be there to do their duty, and everyone will know this by connecting with them through the development of their intuition. Our intuition will be at a higher level in the Age of Aquarius, and more knowledge will be acquired by people. We will develop our thoughts telepathically to communicate with each other. Thus, we will be more aware of our thoughts in the future and be able to control them, for telepathy.

We will learn to develop our brain functions which inspire a lot more intelligence than we realise. As we move up in dimension into Aquarius, it is a new frequency of conscious awareness. Everything that has taken place spiritually has been unnoticed by humans all these years, but it is just that we have not woken up to it. Our awareness and understanding have been switched off, as we have not realised that the spirit world helps with everything that takes place here on Earth.

Scientists, neurologists and other experts in that field are gathering momentum and knowledge about the mind and how the brain works, with its power of developing more and being consciously aware. We are the ones who control the power of our brain, as it is programmed by our thoughts to get things right and under control so that we can communicate telepathically. Getting things right in our head means having beautiful thoughts, to be positive for telepathy. It is only fear that holds us back. Think about how to release fear. If we can release fear and learn to control our thoughts, then it will be safe to communicate telepathically.

There is a lot more we can do with our minds, and as we are heading further into the fifth dimension, we will establish mind over matter to a greater extent. We can get a better connection between matter and the mind, and we can keep becoming better integrated with its potential. With this, we can have the understanding of matter to connect us with everything that we need and are keen to have, and what is necessary for us to have, on the spiritual side, and also with what is worthy and meaningful going into our golden age. Some people think that matter is separate, but it is really connected.

What our perception is of what we think is going to happen is what we receive.

CHAPTER 16

AN INDIVIDUALITY CONNECTION

Being an individual does not mean being separate. Individuality is when a single person or thing has their own way of developing. Something that is separate is something that is not connected to other things. Identifying what is individual and what is separate is hard. If you were to put any two things together, would they actually have an individual or separate connection? It depends. If you think something is individual, you need to describe how it connects individually. If you think something is separate, you can go further by learning that everything is connected and therefore nothing is separate. You need to understand that being separate is just an illusion, as in truth everything is connected.

Oneness education will teach that there is no separation at all. But there is doubt about exactly what is individual and what is separate. Now that you understand the full connection of things, from this book and its chapters, you can look at what is essentially going well with your individuality, in regard to understanding how to move along and work together for peace. A wonderful way of looking at it is to recognise what is needed for world peace and knowing that you have to have inner peace with the essential essence that is within yourself. Always remember that your own individual essence within yourself is part of the worldwide essence of the entire population of the world, for creating world peace. The universal essence that is supporting us to obtain world peace, along with your own individual essence that you know well, makes the proceedings towards peace easier and more understandable. This means the individual essence of everyone is connected to world peace, which connects everyone together. The action that is needed to create a peaceful world is in motion.

I have written in these chapters that there is nothing that is separate, but that all is oneness. I have presented to you for your learning, that all things form into connection from individuality, and that they have always been connected, but humans did not know this. Your individual essence makes a contract with the universal world essence.

Loving affection and kindness gives healing and brings us together companionably. Kindness supports people who need healing, so that we can continue becoming increasingly individually connected with the whole. Evidence of what we call 'individuality' is noticed by others around them who want to connect with the individual, so they can use the energy of their thoughts to make a stronger connection with them. There is no doubt that each individual is fully connected to all others. The gain from this is that we have a basis of individuality, and then we see that one person connects to everything else. It is essentially part of my essence to write this book, to give information about how to gain inner peace, and then work from that to have world peace.

Just one individual who is openly spiritual and has an ability to heal others, can have a complete connection to everyone in the world and be joined with them in peace, and this is a privilege and a treat for that individual. That one individual enhances the domino effect, to speed things up for a rapidly increasing number of individuals to also make the same connection. It is a flow that keeps us moving forward together for an expansion of peace.

What is inside each one of us to keep us going?

Is there a gut instinct inside everyone that we can listen to and put greater focus on in a new way, that is beyond what we could ever dream of? Is there a strong religious belief, with a powerful god and messiah to worship, that keeps believers going? Is it that some people have spiritual beliefs with astrology that they follow, that predicts that we are heading towards a better world?

It is the satisfaction that we get from what we believe in that keeps us going in our human lives. Without a belief system that gives us strength in our mind, we would not have the courage to keep living our life. When our spirituality is lifted to a higher vibration, we realise that all individual people and things are actually connected, and we are open to the possibility of oneness.

Education for the new age will confirm that everything is connected. Objects that we use may appear to be individual items, but may have a joint connection, perhaps as in a set. Sometimes however, things can appear to be individually separate, with no connection between them. There is a connection, but it is tricky to explain. In a set of items, individual pieces have the same value, but only if it is a set that has been given to you that has meaning for you, as you want to have that set as a collection. If the set has no meaning for you, it would be different.

If you have three clear drinking glasses which are the same size and colour, then this is considered by you to be a set. The three glasses would not always be connected if they are side by side and not touching each other, or when you are using them to drink from, but only when they are stored away in the cupboard. The glasses are a physical item which are made of spiritual energy, and all the energy around them is connected to them, and this energy is part of the wellbeing of the universe. This identifies the unity between both worlds, the spiritual and the physical. In the physical world there is an illusion that everything surrounding us is separate, but we are progressing individually on our own pathway, knowing our own essence, and the universal essence.

Oneness cannot be understood in the third dimension and will not be properly understood until the fifth dimension. In fifth-dimensional reality this understanding strengthens our oneness connection, as we are working together. Civilised stability worldwide will be enhanced by combining with all races and cultures to heal the karma of our differences. We know that our differences are individual and not separate, as I have clearly explained the difference between individuality and separateness. What do we know about the word 'together', and how it relates to connection? Together is the word used when two or more things meet up or are in a group, whilst the word 'connection' is used when things join with each other. I am sure you will notice the difference between them. You create an illusion in your mind that things are separate, but oneness education teaches you that all is connected. Everything is connected to you, which brings you that companionship of caring and love.

Within yourself, your own essence has its job to do, and that is what you are here for, and in the outer world your job is to use, and perform with, your own essence, and this is essential for world peace to arrive. Connecting with universal energy helps us know what to do, to work in with, and support each other. The universe's 100% support tactfully charms and persuades us to use our energy to do what is right, and this support is essential to us.

In the Age of Aquarius that we are now in, the children of the new generation who are arriving are inspired to know how to work with us and help us. They have been born into Aquarian energy, into the light of the new age, that shifts and transforms their consciousness. These children are admired for the knowledge they have, from being reincarnated in this strong new era. They will use their essence of why they have come here, to help us, without delay, to know the strategies we must cooperate on in the new age, and how to put them into effect. It is certain to benefit the older generation when they let go and realise that the new age children are wise and helpful. People will listen to the Aquarian-age children when they know they are brighter than the older generation and can help us out.

The incoming of the new age is growing in strength the more the days go by, and it is welcoming the higher entities of human beings reincarnating on Earth as children, to help us enter the new age of peace. There are a lot of degrading comments made by adults about the higher entities coming in, as they think children do not know much and are not as smart as adults. But often children know more and are smarter than adults and they know what to do. The highly evolved children of the new age are being born on Earth to protect us, and to make us aware that we are connected, so that there is no further need for war in the Age of Aquarius. Peace and love in this Aquarian age will stop all fighting, and it will be a thing of the past. We will be fully aware of what the world is meant to be like, in this present moment, of being at the crossroads of transferring war into peace.

This is an amazing time to let go of revenge, have mercy towards those who are violent, and to have forgiveness in your communities and families. Forgiveness is appreciated as people live out their essence in their daily lives. Eliminating violence, that is in our lives from the news media coverage, dissolves confusion so that procedures to expand peace efforts are organised and put into effect. Then we can have the perspective of turning the corner to live a life of enjoyment and peace. There will be a rush to joyfully fulfill the orders and arrangements that will allow us to live freely, the way that we want to, enjoying our connections. Everybody will be pleased with the quality of the connection, and this accompanies everything that the people do with their abilities, when performing their actions.

It is essential for people to behave rightly with their essence, moving forward to obtain wellbeing, and to live out what is rightfully meant to be, to have the best result for peace. Thoughtful inspiration is needed, to negate the effect of wars that prevent the wellbeing and inner peace of humans, as once humans have inner peace, this guarantees that we will have peace on a much larger scale.

There is a lot of controversy about attaining worldwide peace as some do not think it is possible because of the continuous wars. Confusion is dominant and needs to be ended; until this happens, we will not have inner peace, as it is not possible.

Government support with funding to other countries that they have an alliance with, to help them out, strengthens peace. The funding is very helpful to other countries. Government support is vital when the order from the universe with Aquarius is so profound and includes the consensus of people to do the best for peace satisfactorily without being distracted.

Important benefits of watching and listening to news reports is that you can see what is happening, whether it is positive or negative, and the effect of this on the alignment of the news reading. Listeners are happy when they hear a positive news item, as it changes their thoughts to produce a positive outcome for peace. That process involves collaboration with everyone, which builds momentum and creates a snowball effect. Listeners must latch onto the fact that the only way to get to peace is through positive things happening and then taking steps to collaborate.

The main commentary from this book, and from other information you have heard, gives you a real perception of a delivery of peace amongst everyone on Earth.

Government departments need to begin by having annual meetings that are not made public, about the goal of peace. Without a system of communication between governments to resolve issues, and without the support of evolved spiritual beings, there would not be any way of having peace, as there would be no one with the intelligence or ability to develop it.

Unification has to be from the standpoint of connecting science and spirituality, with proof that combines the two sides, so we can collaborate to understand the phenomena of what is taking place. With religion being phased out and that connection cut off, we can see the exact connection between science and spirituality from a clear viewpoint. Removing religious knowledge created doubts in the minds of many believers, but science and spirituality ideas were right. The growth of both science and spirituality brings to our notice the contrast between them in their beliefs, which gives us more knowledge about each of them when they are combined. These beliefs become known when science and spirituality are put together. When you have some knowledge about science, as well as some knowledge about spirituality, and you combine your knowledge of them both, then you can see the sequence ahead that results from this combination. For example, from the science of matter and the spirituality of matter, we will really begin to know what matter is.

Religious people are recognising that they have more of a connection with science and spirituality, whereas they had no real connection in their religion, due to wars and religious behaviours using control and fear. This is why religion has dropped in numbers and is falling out of favour.

Citizens are gathering together with others in their daily lives to understand science and spirituality. Our perception in our mind's eye is always worthwhile using, to help find world peace, as that is our ongoing goal. All beneficial positive events are leading us to our goal. There needs to be a lot of positive expectations throughout the world to the extent that is needed to achieve our aim. The Age of Aquarius is hard to see ahead of us because it is camouflaged by the confusion of the fourth-dimensional crossroads. You know when to get off the roundabout of where we are going now in the fourth dimension, and it is joyful once you know you are on the right track, and you keep going along it. We are right at the crossroads to another dimension in a higher reality that is achievable, in which world peace will be given to us by the universe when we work together and support each other. We all need to learn what it is like to live in a peaceful world with no war, living in harmony. We will be meeting together with compassion, and interacting with each other, firstly as an individual, and secondly as a connection to work with.

Similarly, a connection with each other works out well both individually and together, as it is apparent that the difference between individuality and separation decreases even further. The way to go about it is to have a connection between what you do, and what we all do.

We are all gathered together to learn with our own essence and the Earth's essence, to strengthen within us what we need on a cellular basis. What is within us plays together with the action being taken out in the world, to obtain what we are working for. You must be thorough in your plans, actions and interactions to get the results you want. The most upheaval for people is when they have to work towards having companionship in their community, as well as going out on a larger basis into the wider world. With all communities in the world working together, we know we can have faith that the peace sign is raised permanently, because we can guarantee peace.

There is no doubt that we are living our way to a whole new world. Peacekeepers from the United Nations unite us all, along with government funding and agreements with citizens and other governments. Formal agreements must be made to enhance government funding to help citizens and to help other countries and their citizens.

Our loving task is to have joy in everything we do, which makes our life easier, and by enjoying our life and working together, we will have worldwide joy.

All the governments will put everything into action that is right and true for all the citizens, and this extravaganza of support for the citizens will create the best alignment for joy in the world. This government support is ongoing to the crowds of citizens who have the same ideas and think the same way. It is a profound privilege for these community members to work communally with others of like mind, and they will recognise this privilege that they have.

The onwards motion supports us all in uniting to get the peace we have all wanted for such a long time but have been unable to accomplish. Knowing, from the words of this chapter, that everything is individual but not separate, brings up the connection to achieve what we want. The compromise of meeting halfway, of once believing and now knowing, (where the believing and the knowing once met halfway), has ended, as our knowing is now taking over. To reach the outcome we want, we will follow the well-thought-out process to do the job that we know is right. We must be aware that the quality of our behaviour affects our outcome, therefore we must maintain appropriately convincing attitudes in our conduct. What is meant to happen will progress here on Earth, with the result that peace will ensue from everyone combining their abilities. Our organising must be purposeful with good ideas that we know are worthwhile. Progress must have precision with acute beneficial results, to move ahead in a substantial way.

The realisation that we must figure out what to release and what is in the way of our goal, helps us to know we have to release our confusion. We all know what is happening by the results we see. Everything that is happening with everyone in the world is being noticed by us, and with this recognition we can see what place it has in the outcome, and we see what we have to change, and then it automatically moves forward. We have to know what the corporations, government and citizens are doing to change things.

Every one of us, in our individual essence of seeing world peace and what we have to do to fulfill this, has the combination with the world essence to fulfill all knowing that we must step into the light and love of the new world. We cannot let the light and love come to us; we have to go into it. It may seem as if some people's essence does not fit in with world peace, but they will still be invited to have the outcome of peace. Some things have to get worse before peace arrives, and this will be these people's essence to be involved in the worse things that happen.

Every possibility can happen. Each outcome has a probability of occurring. You want the best possibility to happen, but there can still be issues that get worse. It is important to be aligned with the extravaganza, with its large energy like a large celebration that brings us all together, to live the best life that we could ask for in the Age of Aquarius.

The old beliefs must go, in order for the new age to develop connection, with the enjoyment of living in the hands of peace. Our modern-day spirituality is influenced by our kindness to others, to share the prosperity. Each individual has their own thoughts about what each of them has to do, and these thoughts become known when we step into Aquarius. We are leaving the era of "I believe" for the era of "I know". The meaning is that everyone has their own individual essence that will lead them into peacefulness and oneness connection in the Age of Aquarius, and we will all be able to stay on the same timeline with what we are doing.

Some people think we are all separate, so they think there is a division between separation and individuality, but when we all come to realise our connection, there is no such thing as separateness. The barriers, where people thought we were separate, have been done away with, as the teachings in our incoming new age have proof that we are all connected.

CHAPTER 17

CRIME AND MERCY

Crimes are committed daily by lawbreakers, who will receive a punishment in the justice system of their country if they are caught. This does not necessarily prevent them from committing more crimes when they have served their sentence. Innocent people may be charged with crimes they did not commit, and be imprisoned, due to an injustice being done to them. The range of crimes committed is vast. With the use of technology and electronics in current times, financial crimes have increased. Criminals are clever at defrauding and stealing money from unsuspecting people, even though security measures are continually being improved and tightened.

The more that humanity matures and becomes more grown up and connected, the less crime there will be, and the more people will have mercy, along with forgiveness. Mercy is forgiveness, leniency, help and compassion towards the wrongdoer. As humanity matures, we will understand criminals and gather knowledge about crimes, and we will have mercy. Learning acceptance of other people in your everyday life will allow the ability within yourself to have forgiveness, as you will have a one understanding of the connection between us all.

We will have an increased tolerance of crime; we will fight it, while understanding that there are always reasons behind crimes that are committed, and with understanding and connection we will have forgiveness. This shows us where we are at the crossroads of turning over our state of separateness to what we understand by connection. When we understand about connection, in the makeover (or changeover), and agree on it, we can make the most of where we are. The arrangements set out by the universe and ourselves are that we work on our thoughts to improve them, so we can walk along the pathway of enlightenment.

The maturity of humanity will improve things so that there is fairness to everyone, with organised humanitarianism and the support this gives to the world. People are oblivious to this maturity of humanity at first, as the crime rate is so high and people are focused on ways to reduce it. The purpose of crime is to highlight what is right and wrong with the law, and for society to demand that their government make stricter laws to protect the population from crime. Stricter penalties will be needed for crime, and stronger safety measures and security, with rights being incorporated into the law.

The prosecution can be harsh on crime in some countries, with harsh punishments. Innocent people are sometimes punished due to an injustice being done to them. Throughout human history there has been crime, but with the new universal introspection we can agree to stop crime. It will work when we have an attitude of forgiveness toward others and work with security issues to keep the population safe, as well as being kind to each other and ensuring everyone receives a fair share of prosperity. Understanding the law of cause and effect resolves crime issues; what you do comes back to you. Realising what you know about yourself and what you have to do to successfully make agreements with those in your community, will fulfill the hope for peace that you have within yourself. Humanity will mature when it realises the human race is fully connected, which is when they will have forgiveness, and will take action to accomplish what they have to do – bring out world peace while realising the wholeness connection.

Crime will be ended, and humanity would have matured enough to behave in a united manner, coming together to maturely work well together with a peaceful mindset. Our mind, when aligned with humanitarianism, is very powerful, and we achieve a lot when we know we are connected, as we work like a human hospital, by healing one another's wounds. There is nothing like being together and working together for the new world, in a way that is significant for peace, and being inspired to know exactly how to stop crime. When people have forgiveness, it creates peace amongst all humans, as an attitude of forgiveness creates inner peace, which brings outer peace into all areas of life. We all need peace in our minds to be clear about exactly what is right as we are working together.

Walking forward and marching on for peace uses the energy to make progress at a faster rate to achieve the advancement that we set out to do, with our perspective of what needs to be done. This is opening up the way for us to notice the energy and order of the universe, with the people in their communities being grounded (centered and stable) by their alignment with their wellbeing. Onward momentum is taking place as we collectively go through the stages towards peace. All movement is activated energy from Earth's people moving ahead to a stable situation in their new lifestyle. There is no doubt in our awareness that crime is happening, and being wise with our thoughts, we can have a makeover to be surprisingly beneficial, in helping out generously in the peace making. This automatically goes with humanitarianism, as helping to solve crime brings joy into the hearts of human beings, because they release tension. The more stress-free that humans are, the easier it is for them to work together and to form important collaborations with trust, being honoured to do the duty of putting things right.

Believing in ourselves creates trust, to know the standards in the matured core of our wellbeing. Being stress-free in our lives, whilst finding our inner peace in our mind, gives us presence in knowing our way to foretell global harmony. With this knowledge in our minds, we learn that to have ongoing peace with the perspective of the life we have created with our mind, we must realise the core connection that the universe understandably and automatically provides for us.

There is no disconnection in the joinery of reality, and no breaking point, as it is not possible. Reality is real, and every bit of progress from just a single thought joins all the particles and connects them. The ongoing mutual trust with our advisors and leaders means having a say in what we all need, and about where we are, on moving ahead towards what we all desire. Releasing tension through meditation is needed, to be stress-free, and it is seen as being normal in the community to release tension this way.

To be stress-free, the most known way is through having the skills to remain at peace with whatever is happening around you, by:

1. Being with yourself. Your individual essence working with inner peace in your head.
2. Being with others. All working together for peace.

The best situation is when we are always working together, knowing what is happening for peace, and that this fills our life, giving us our own biggest achievement.

Our behaviour is the biggest clue that makes us recognise that what is inside us, and what goes out from us, is achieving our aim. Challenges will be given to us, to dive ahead very strongly and make good progress, so we can see what is ahead, as well as feeling like we are ahead, with the stability of grounding in our physical body. The stability of the Earth plane gives you the ability to progress with your energy and actions that you have put out. Preparing your life to be a life worth living with the biggest achievement and the best possible outcome, is the mature way of being stress-free. This is precisely the best way forward, like you could never imagine! This puts you into place for the outcome you deserve, and what you are supposed to get in your life. What is in your life is the present state (of your life), working together with the essence of ourselves, and the essence of the world put together. There is joy in your essence in working through what it is doing, with its consistent presence, building your skills and success from what happens in your life. When you have your own essence and the world essence, the way is there for you to follow with your focus of what you have to achieve.

Always follow your gut feeling, as it is inspired to be true for you, but if it is not true for some reason, you can still listen to it and confront it, asking why it did not work out for you according to plan. There are always reasons. Your gut feeling prompts you to act on your purpose, to fulfill your essence with the duty required from you. Maybe you did not try hard enough, or it was not the right time, and you have free will as to whether you will go with your gut feeling. Other people's free will may also interfere.

Always have strong thought-out procedure in the system in society for solving crime and be supportive of the government in this. When we have strong thoughts to put action into procedures, the universe, that is so strongly welcoming with its support, will support us back in achieving that.

It is exciting to think that crime will be no more, as that is a fast step towards our goal. The faster that massive crime is resolved, then the faster we can move forward in the development of the lives that we want and feel entitled to have. Greed is prevalent everywhere in the world, a continual wanting for more money. Until financial systems are established giving all of us worldwide a fair share of income, negative types of people will continue to commit theft as they cannot stop themselves. As I have mentioned before in this book, there will be stronger technology that can give pure proof of crime, heaven, and oneness connection that will be beneficial and supportive in bringing us together. The technology will be so advanced that there will be no chance of errors, and the advanced security will do its job correctly; it is so technically advanced that it is 100% accurate.

If your situation is that you yourself have committed a crime, do not feel guilty; it is just part of what is meant to happen with your essence. You have to forgive yourself for doing the crime, and the other person also has to forgive you. Offenders know they have done something bad when they commit a crime, and they may have remorse, but they will be taught not to feel guilty, as it is part of their essence and what they are supposed to do. Others will be taught to be kinder and to forgive you through the connection of oneness teaching.

We have to look up to higher dimensions, to come together with awareness so we are prepared to be working together, to do away with confusion. The energy of confusion is invisible, even though it is with us all the time. Once we manage to dissolve confusion, our civilisation will know what to work on, that is right for peace. We already know what is right, but because of confusion, we are being held back from companionship.

What happens with crime and mercy is that those who have committed crimes are often sorry and beg for mercy. This makes the victim and the jury system more lenient and forgiving, if this is allowed by the court, although they still want the offender to be punished. There needs to be stricter rules in prison so that offenders receive counselling to cure their mindset, to stop them committing crimes. People who cannot forgive others for crimes, often are the ones who beg for mercy when they themselves commit a crime.

Fairness can come with mercy, as people beg for help, and someone helps them; then something better returns to that someone who helped them out, due to the law of cause and effect.

The wrongdoer may serve a prison term and receive class teachings in prison to help him/her, perhaps with counselling as well, so they will not reoffend. The way out of all of this is to develop by living your life better. Then you redevelop, so that you make full progress working with others for a better world, while knowing the strength within you.

When lawbreakers are in prison, they may actually be given cures for their mental disorders and illnesses (including childhood trauma). This will be in the future when they develop cures, so that when they are released from prison they will not reoffend. Counselling and medication will be the cures, as there will be new prescription medications that will actually cure all mental afflictions. Once there are cures, we will know what is right, in our minds, to achieve peace.

When we all know oneness connection we will have equal power, so that we will be safe in our companionship together. It will be easy-going in our day-to-day lives as we lengthen and strengthen with our equal power that makes things better. People will not be able to abuse their power as we will all have an equal amount, and we will use it appropriately in a way that is right.

We will move forward with universal power, and once arrived at the outcome, it will become part of us, as we will have full knowledge and consciousness of the power of our thoughts, and what will happen from them (as the energy of our thoughts comes back to us.)

We will learn to feed on the universal essence as it is becoming stronger with the new energy that we know about with Aquarius. Feeding on the universal essence is when the universe gives us its essence, incorporating it into every single one of us and making it part of us, just from its powerful energy, so that we can tap into it and draw on it, for our use. The powerful universal essence displayed to us in its extreme force is part of our essence, and on an individual basis this will be incorporated into us as we all work together for what is best.

The world essence combines with the universal support for all living things on the earthly realm; humans, animals and all creatures, as they all have an essence too.

Our knowing would have matured so much that it will be hard to believe how we treated others so badly some time ago. What is essential and right, is to keep going on in daily life and to be aware of awful crimes, but to know we are coming into ways of stopping them as soon as possible.

There is terrible killing in the Middle East and in some parts of Africa, for example, but things will take their course to overcome the killing, as it is a natural part of life that things have to come to an end.

A lot of pressure is on the world, with the bombs and destruction, which causes pressure on human beings to get things right within each one of us. Ongoing destruction keeps confusion in place, and we are holding back and not getting settled inside ourselves, so we do not know what to do. The bad people who are causing the destruction keep going, and the good people notice what they are doing and take action to stop them. No matter how hard people try to stop destruction and crime, it does not seem as if we are getting anywhere. Until we are past the crossroads, and we are completely in the Age of Aquarius, it seems as if there is no chance of anything better, as the confusion is still there in dominant control, and holding its place.

Crime will continue, while mercy with forgiveness towards criminals will increase from now on, and from there we will achieve much stronger steps towards global unity. People will understand more about crime and mercy, and they will be able to forgive criminal acts.

Because everything is oneness connection, crime and mercy combines and merges into one, along with everything else. Crime is such a big issue as it includes murder, rape and other serious unlawful acts. With forgiveness, it will work into one and end up eliminating crime as it merges with oneness. Crime will be quickly dissolved, and mercy will be justified with the oneness connection. Crime and mercy, when put together, comes into one and dissolves crime. When crime and mercy merge, and mercy eliminates the crime, then there will be no more mercy, as it will not be needed, therefore it fades away.

CHAPTER 18

TEARS AND LAUGHTER

What do you think of this? Are tears and laughter the best medicine for accessing the answers inside you? It may seem a bit hard to establish this as a fact, and I know it really makes you think. I can guarantee that laughter is the best medicine; all you have to do is start laughing and see what happens. You will be filled with joy, with tears coming out of your eyes. It lightens your mood and your vibration rises, and this even happens if it is a fake laugh, as the brain cannot tell any difference in the sound.

Do something you enjoy and have fun – watch funny movies, gather together to tell jokes and funny stories, or try laughter yoga classes. It may seem harder and not so beneficial doing a fake laugh, so if that is the case, place yourself in a situation that creates real laughter, to lift your spirits.

This may seem silly or even crazy to some of you people, however, laughter is the trick to release everything necessary from the brain that has been trapped and is causing headaches. Painful headaches are terrible, but the brain reacts to your laughter, whether it is a fake laugh or a real laugh, by releasing the stuck feelings. It can be hard to try new things, but laughing on your own for the first time can be the best way to see what happens.

Tears and laughter on a regular basis can be a unique way of helping yourself, by releasing negativity from deep inside you that is blocking you and holding you back in your life. Tears help to release the hurts and any pain inside you that is lingering and needs to be released.

When people cry, sometimes they can be ridiculed by others, with name-calling, and told to toughen up and be brave. This can result in them suppressing their hurt and keeping it all inside themselves, due to others' expectations for them to be quiet.

The reason we need to laugh and cry is to release all the old negative stuff inside us so that we can have inner peace. What is important for people to know is that laughter is the best medicine for healing as it clears anything that is inside you that is trapped. Laughter naturally unleashes happiness and a state of wellbeing. This happy wellbeing may flow on to others, because the strength and enthusiasm of it may improve their state of mind, as there is a connection between us all.

We have to move forward by trying different things to see what makes you laugh, whether it is tickling one another, feeling good about yourself, playing your favourite game, or anything else that cheers you up. Different things will apply for different people.

Preconceived outcomes happen when you know that the negativity and blockages will be cured by laughter that works as a medicine. You need to think about what is stuck inside you and how to release it, and how to use laughter to do this. Attuning yourself with laughter has the right vibrational sound to cure all negative energy throughout the body.

Our beliefs about happiness are becoming more widely known by the public and will become ingrained with the new world. We need laughter for that to happen.

The use of colour can cheer you up, for instance, wearing clothes with more colour, or having more colourful items inside your home, or putting more colour in your garden or your artwork.

Spiritual leaders will open up more places to hold laughter classes. The more positive laughter that takes place, the better, and the more the merrier.

Releasing negativity in our minds and bodies activates the codes in our DNA. These codes need to be cleansed of negativity and activated to create a higher vibration in us. Laughter medicine cleanses the codes, which means that the cells are connecting in our body as they cleanse, and they connect up to a higher vitality.

My own preconceived outcome with laughter will drive people to realise they know that what is indeed dissolved within them is all the negative emotions such as hatred, anger, rage and fear, as well as resentment, doubt, worry, despair and many others including guilt, shame, jealousy, bitterness, depression, frustration, sadness, annoyance and anxiety.

There are certain happy people who are always cheerful and laughing, and this affects others positively as their energy is powerful.

If we can see something that may be for a better world or a worse world, we start worrying and agonising, feeling as though we are fighting within ourselves, to understand it because it is confusing. When you are confused, it can start a fight inside yourself or with others and it can be emotional, but an alternative is to laugh it off.

Some people have a common saying: "just laugh it off and it will go away." It may not always appear to work out that way but trying this method may be preferable to feeling bad or depressed about it. Fighting inside yourself is caused by confusion and agonising over different courses of action.

The joy of laughter that you have in a laughter yoga class, is that everyone's laughter supports everyone else because it causes companionship, and the monetary fee supports the teacher. The more laughter yoga classes that are being held, the more income the teacher makes. More classes help more people, transforming their negativity. This utilises the facilities more, such as halls, community centers, conference rooms, and similar venues. The leaders of laughter yoga will safely bring everybody together, sharing the same power to connect us all with centered humanity.

Laughter can help to transform the frequency of meditation to a clearer sense, which lets our brain know we are moving forward to a much higher frequency of spirituality. Once we have a clear mind from laughter, we can meditate better, which will help us see how to clear our negativity for inner peace, and we will know how to transform the physical world into peace. With a clear mind we can interpret any messages we receive clearly, and our brain cells connect up more too. Laughter lifts you to a higher frequency, and you could even laugh when you are meditating to inspire you more.

The healing effect of laughter works like a slow-release time capsule, that takes place over time and heals everything in your mind. Then, when we work together, the universe creates a domino effect of the healing in large groups of people, releasing through laughing, that helps us work interactively for a shared goal.

Laughter will free up your mind. It will clear the negativity and create healing so that we can carry out our occupations, working unitedly for a new age outcome in the world.

It does not matter if the laughter is real or fake, as the brain cannot tell the difference between the two. The receptors in the brain that receive the laughter sounds clear the baggage out so that we can have inner peace. That is freedom worth fighting for. Just start laughing and see what happens, and if you do not notice any difference, perhaps try joining with a large group and laughing aloud with them, as the energy of the group will cheer you up more.

There is no fear in being stuck, and as we go into the new world everyone will be released from their stagnation, by working with the higher fifth-dimensional energy. The support of that fifth-dimensional energy and all the energetic support we give each other, will cure all feelings of being stuck at a much faster rate.

Laughing yourself silly raises you to the same level of alignment as fifth-dimensional reality. The more that people are healed by laughing, the more purified they will become by moving into the new age. Purification, in the golden age, means that there will be no disease, no negativity and no one will be stuck. When we work together, each dawn will bring a better day. If we have laughter and become much happier people, it will speed up the frequency for us to get into the fifth dimension at a much faster pace.

We will be a lot more aware of our thoughts in our mind, and what we imagine, as well as knowing it will develop into real life reality just from our thinking.

Our governments will apply rules that are more spiritual, to get things right, and to change old laws that were not working out for the better. The laughter is capturing a feeling of being more spiritual, along with an understanding of this, and is endorsed by others' support. All the tearful laughter we have together will bring a restful state within ourselves, as it releases all negativity and hurt inside, to make us purely cleansed.

When we all have inner peace settled within us, we will know and identify, by locking into our awareness with clarity, the meaning of inner peace and how it feels. Anyone who does not want to make the effort to go ahead with this will be helped by others. When we understand the obstacles I have explained in these chapters, from the point of view of changing the old way of seeing things into the new way of seeing things, it brings more coordination between us as it eliminates competition.

The truth speaks for itself when we see everyone contributing and putting into effect the agreements they make, keeping in line with the support of the universal order, which is the energy of everything connected and the frequency and awareness of it. The universal order becomes stronger as a result of this. Universal energy and the spirit world are reaching out to us more strongly, so we can meet up with the realisation that we must act together to agree on what we want to achieve, and how to keep everything right on track towards our goal.

The basic proposition for what has to be arranged and organised at the crossroads must be right and on track to appear admirable, as interception to block the wars increases. Then we can come together in partnership with others with the duty to increase the unity and prepare oneness.

The spiritual world is coming together with the material world to support an improvement in the loving kindness of humanity. Participation in loving kindness has us moving ahead as we enjoy more laughter, taking precautions to ensure we give the impression that we value the tears and laughter that you bravely release out of you to have inner peace, and realising it is joyful to cry. This creates harmony within you, which delivers worldwide peace with everyone contributing to the world order.

We are actually very aware subconsciously that the universe is connected with us, and when we are working together, and we know what is right, it is changing from the manual formation, where we have to do the work ourselves, to an automatic formation, where the universe takes over for us and works it out for us. The universe automatically takes over and guides people subconsciously, and they do not even realise the universe is guiding them.

As we understand this connection with the universe, our fears will fade away more. People think of the worst-case scenario of what could happen, such as a nuclear holocaust, a big natural disaster, or becoming homeless, and this causes them fear and worry. Some types of fear are necessary to keep ourselves physically safe from danger or injury, so that we will be careful.

Laughter helps to reduce many fears, but we still have to feel fearful about some things for our own safety. With the support of the universe, we will have laughter and adjust to what we know is right and wrong about fear.

Our collaboration with the universe is justified, we feel, as we notice how economically the support works in an automatic motion rather than a manual motion. If we were not consciously aware of the power of the universe, we would not realise it is so economically supportive, meaning that it all flows well and works out, and is for the better.

To get justice for inner peace, you have to know to laugh and cry, to release toxins which have built up over your lifetime from fear, which has overshadowed the love inside you, so that you have forgotten about it. Ongoing laughter will find the way to what is inside inner peace. The opposite to fear is love, and if you dissolve fear with all your tears and laughter, you are on the right track to discover what is within inner peace.

The positivity of the light overpowers the negativity of the dark. By knowing the power of the universe, we can eliminate all negativity from our minds to know pure love in the way that is beneficial to us. This is transforming all negativity into positive energy so we can understand there is only love, both in the material world and the spiritual world.

There is now only one thing that is the answer to what is within inner peace:

PURE LOVE.

The light is so pure that it is Pure Love.

The positive energy cannot go backwards to negativity from where it came, as the negativity has been eliminated with the empowerment of all human beings and the universe.

Proof of pure love is proof of heaven, which eliminates the negativity that is only a location in our mind.

CHAPTER 19

AGEING WITH JOY

Joy transcends the age barrier, affecting quality of life and mental and physical health. Social connections and participation in meaningful activities brings out joy. Connecting positively with others is important for our wellbeing as we reach the milestones of older age.

In numerology, the calculation of numbers speak for themselves, and the proof of this is in the Age of Aquarius, which has new universal awareness and order. As we constantly notice the new frequency of Aquarius, our enthusiasm increases. The wisdom of Aquarius informs us all to move ahead with capability. Every step we take in our daily lives here on Earth has tremendous consequences and impact that affects us all according to what we put out. As we move further into Aquarius, the confusion will dissipate very quickly, giving us positive intuition for a better Earth. As we head into the fifth dimension we will understand about the confusion, which will help eliminate it.

The ageing process happens naturally, and we have to go with the flow, as we have no choice. It can seem as if there are worrying or threatening things ahead, outside of our control, that could happen in the world, and this brings fear in the third eye of our mind, thereby holding back our perception of a good outcome to look forward to. The fear makes us doubt our knowledge so that it seems like there is no hope for a better future.

Financial balance is needed, for everyone to receive their fair share without causing conflicts, and this may be tricky to safely create this balance. As the universe spits out the old and brings in the new, it supports us by doing away with confusion, so that we are on a better basis. The track forward can be very confusing as it appears that everything is getting worse rather than better, but things have to collapse before they get better, because we are at the crossroads. Those who are ageing here on the Earth plane have in their mind's eye the new welcoming move into Aquarius.

The complex ageing process necessitates lessons around learning how to have joy and letting go of what we have been holding onto, our past baggage. Ageing with joy is our aim and goal as we wake up to what we want to achieve. An onslaught of negativity from wars, conflicts and natural disasters will get us changing and transforming more quickly to move into the golden age. Joy automatically transforms the ageing process into happiness and wellbeing. When fear is eliminated, there will only be love and joy. Older adults will have joy from following the younger people, often their own children, and receiving the news and teachings from them.

Cures for health issues will assist those who are ageing to feel joy, and reversing of the ageing process will be done by the medical field as time goes by. Anti-gravity devices will mean that life will not be so hard on us, and we will be connected with the spiritual side.

Lightworkers and others are sending positive love to the evil and negativity that is happening in the world. From sending love to evil, we develop happiness in our heart and soul for our wellbeing. We must contemplate how to get into alignment with the universe, to manifest our ideas that are worthy of implementation.

In a sign of recognition of what is taking place, all those citizens and governments who have access to the central databases will fill them with the real truth of all happenings. Anything negative or for the purpose of evil in databases will be thrown out, so that good content that we know to be true can be recorded. The old businesses are collapsing to bring in the new age, so that everything that happens with people is fair. As the new age comes in, it sweeps all the old age stuff away. Those who are against the new age finally realise we have to make the world a better place, with everyone receiving a fair share of everything.

Let us take a good look at the human ageing process and ageism. Ageism is prejudice and discrimination against people because of their age. This can have a big effect. It is a natural thing that younger people think they know better than those who are older than them. Older citizens can become physically weaker, and in some cases may also lose their mental strength as well, and this causes discrimination. Ageism has a negative impact. Aged people have been treated differently for a long time, although the word 'ageism' was not used until 1969, when a psychiatrist initiated the term because of the discrimination and prejudice against older people. Older age affects the physical and mental health of people, and eventually the older population will die in the material world and pass on to the spiritual world. Age discrimination will continue until people know we are all connected. There are negative attitudes towards older age and the ageing process, with negative stereotypes and discriminatory practices against older citizens. We can fight against ageism by understanding ingrained attitudes about older people. Focusing on the positive things about the older population would help, for example, their wisdom and life experience, the volunteer work that they do, the way they help out in the community and being valued grandparents. We need to make a oneness connection to others by having a caring attitude and developing loving kindness. Stereotypes should be rejected; the focus should be on the individual, their positive traits and their uniqueness.

The outer group of younger people are the ones with discriminatory attitudes, and they do not want to change, while the inner group of young people care and want to move forward by eliminating ageism. These two groups must connect and overcome discrimination and negative attitudes, and work things out with an attitude of oneness.

Social discrimination and prejudice are not okay, where younger people expect those who are older to stay in their own age group socially and not mix with those who are young. It is best to ask for help if you are being discriminated against, and you can seek help and advice from senior citizen agencies, social workers and legal advocates.

We have trust that the oneness connection will cure ageism. When ageism is cured, it will bring joy to people and make Earth a better place for older citizens. Ending ageism strengthens the mind, body and soul to know we can work together in communities with no discrimination, having kindness for each other in social gatherings or groups. Older and younger folks are capable of going to the same events with a positive attitude, bringing everyone together on a safe basis without discrimination. We are going into a new world with no ageism, and with the oneness connection. It will not be necessary to uphold human rights, as we will know exactly what is right for working together.

People are occupied with the things in their lives that have meaning for them; working through their own essence, which is part of the world essence, that contributes to the changing of life on Earth to a new era, bringing us all together as one to work for world peace. Everyone knowing the oneness connection means everyone will trust the process of working together, to make progress that is exactly right, regarding the entire ageing process. A full understanding of what is right and wrong will be known by everyone, along with the calculations of what is needed to receive overall peace. Our minds will be centered with focused awareness so we can interact in our lives and gain the highest benefit, to the highest standard. There will not be any negativity holding us back to keep us stuck, so we will move ahead in a beneficial flow. The oneness connection, from people's learning, has transformed their ingrained old beliefs to what is now their new beliefs, that contribute to a global system of peace that is essential.

Our lives will be gentler when we intentionally practice loving kindness, with consideration and tactfulness towards one another, to nurture healing among us. In the new age lifestyle, compromise and giving joy provides what is necessary for our wellbeing. The universe supports everyone with their individual thoughts, but the leaders have the power with their own individual thoughts, to persuade everyone else to be involved in helping the progress. The leaders will benefit by moving everyone ahead. These leaders are trusted because of the oneness connection, and this trust is their source of power; this empowers them to work beneficially for world peace. The support from the leaders will keep everyone on the same right timeline so we can work together for peace and go into the fifth dimension together. Humans will grow up with new oneness education and will know exactly how to behave going into the new world, and they will support the older ones with this as well.

Whenever you put everything together with joy, people can collaborate and understand better. It is simply a three-letter word that is astounding; it is a short word that stands out and has the same meaning as happiness, and is just JOY in itself. Taking action by moving forward in the best way accomplishes every goal in a joyful way. There is no better way to put it, except to say that enjoyment is just having fun in what you are doing. We need joy to achieve inner peace, peace on Earth, and a peaceful atmosphere. With joy you can manage everything, and you feel pride and excitement just by feeling that emotion of joy. Everyone wants a fair share of joy to enhance their lives. Speaking the word 'joy' aloud as in an affirmation that can be repeated over and over, puts power into the words. Other words such as happiness, peace, harmony, bliss and delight are similar to joy and add up to a team of happy words.

Every bit of the ageing process needs to be recognised and valued, to transform our thoughts through learning about ageing. Everyone will grow older one day in their life. They can learn what may happen to them physically, mentally and socially, including how to deal with it and cope with it. They need to know where to go for help if they need it, to avoid being socially isolated and lonely due to poor health or mobility issues. To reset the ageing process, everyone must take part and interact in activities that add to their wellbeing. Life is worth living, even though you have to go through the ageing process, by finding the positives and focusing on them, such as family and social connections.

Introverted people, with that personality trait, are joining in more with the rest of us, which benefits them as then they do not miss out on the help the other older individuals are receiving. The advantage of the introverted ones joining in, is that they are aligning with everybody's wellbeing, and with the transformation to the new world, no one is missing out, as we are all on the same timeline. This inspiring alignment of everybody with our entitlement to world peace, causes us to thrive with wellbeing to complete our destiny in the world. Our thoughts are redeveloping to change our progress so that we are working together for the better, for the world destiny. The government has to have democracy and inclusion of all citizens, and listen to them, to get things right for the betterment of all, as everyone in society is ageing.

The more connection with, and knowledge of, the spiritual world and the universe that we have, the more things will fit into place correctly. When we have proof of heaven, we can go ahead with what we know is right for us to do, following along with the topics in this book and taking action together. Following on from the precise detail that we know from this book and from supportive government data, the connected interaction between the government and citizens will do away with confusion.

Your mind and all your wellbeing will transplant the negative energy out of your body so that you can live a well life. When your mind is positive and all is well, and when confusion is eliminated, the negative energy will work its way out of your body.

You can see clearly what is happening with your intuition, in your mind's eye. To have the courage to do this and use your intuition means doing something different from what is accepted in society as the normal way of doing things.

Our attitudes will change, and we will work together in a spiritually unique way amongst different cultures in society. This spiritual behaviour may seem unusual at first, but we will soon adjust and come together in one cultural way of behaving.

Taking part in this new society will be pleasant for those who are ageing with joy.

CHAPTER 20

MINDFULNESS

Mindfulness will connect you to the point during meditation that supplies you with the best memory for working things out, without judgement of anything or anyone.

When people realise the connection of things, they will know the right way of thinking, and that their thoughts produce what happens in their life. People will learn new skills to control their thoughts and keep them positive. They will teach others these skills, along with the new brain techniques that are developed to help people control their own thoughts, minds and emotions, instead of their thoughts, minds and emotions controlling them.

You realise through your connection that there is only one present, therefore live only in the now with no judgement. There is no up or down, past or future, or any judgement of anything. There is only one center, which is always the present. As there is only one now, there is no left or right, or forward or backward; there is only the illusion of any comparison in the material world.

There will be no judgement when we all turn to spirituality, as we will accept everyone for who they are. When we realise the individual connection, this will place the knowing in the heart of our mind that there will be no further need for judgement.

The challenge is to know how to get into the right timeline for what is meant to happen, but we have to go with universal flow and the support of working together, to create financial equality for all in the Age of Aquarius. When we get into the right timeline, the universe will support us right through to Aquarius. The new world will just come to us from the universal energy, and we will notice the order of it and go into it.

Mindfulness is knowing we can have achievement just by keeping a calm clear mind. By taking positive steps forward and being grounded, centered and aligned, we will have a clear mind that develops in a way that works for us. So instead of us working things out with our mind, our mind works with us.

Linear time works well in the physical world so that things happen in progression. However, in the spiritual world everything is happening at once as there is no time. By going through each day in our lives, we have to live through one present thing at a time, but if our mind is free, then we will be stress-free to succeed in our destiny.

World peace is going to be right upon us, and mindfulness will give it a clear pathway. When we incorporate spirituality on Earth, meditation will be accepted so that we can eternalise coming together to cooperate with group meditations.

As we are human beings living in the material world in the contamination of confusion of fourth- dimensional reality, our human minds feel justified in wanting calmness. With mindfulness, inner peace is enhanced, and introspection with meditation uses the arising thoughts to fulfill you inside even more. This is the alleyway to global peace, as our human minds have the power to project the future to bring about the world we want. The essential essence of the Earth is to have peace, along with open proof of heaven and the level of our connection with it.

The only thing is the NOW, and as we come to realise this when we understand illusion, it enhances what we are seeing in our mind's eye.

There will be mindfulness on how we will obtain absolute proof of heaven, which would eliminate human's fear of 'hell' that restricted our reality in the material world. We will have no fear of transition into the spiritual side, as we know from the proof of the afterlife what it is like. We will understand how humans relate to each other, and the effects and results this has, while the proof of heaven will connect the two sides, spiritual and physical, to us.

We will feel much lighter and brighter in the mindful state of fifth-dimensional reality. This will give us connection to everything as we carry on living with the need for fifth-dimensional oneness.

We are becoming aware, with mindfulness, of what needs to be done. We have a clear sense of wellbeing, from what plays out in meditation, for ourselves. The need for single-mindedness becomes more individual as people have to be focused on the specific goal of peace.

The Buddhist tradition will be incorporated into spirituality as they have a strong focus to maintain inner peace. As an increasing number of people practice mindfulness, peace on Earth will grow, and it will go on to flow from everything that is thought-out and considered in the topics of this book. It is a priority to keep people in touch by informing them collectively about issues being considered.

High energy from the frequency with mindful meditation clears your mind so it is easier to think things over.

Connecting with the accord in the communities, and taking one step at a time, means you can be with mindfulness and go with it, to be clear on all events around you.

Meditation can make your mind so clear that you have no thoughts in your head, only what you are thinking in the present, and there is only one present. Every thought has a tremendous effect because of the universe's 100% playback support. There is guaranteed support from the universe for all those working communally as one on the issues that are the topics of this book. This support locks everything into place with the action of the domino effect, which is thorough and strong enough to support creativeness for peace throughout the world.

Our clear mindfulness brings to our notice the succession planning needed to plan the order in which to do things. To succeed, you have to keep moving on towards your goal, and you need to become aware of your consciousness. Mindfulness gives you a clear mind so you know exactly what you are doing, and you can think straight. Mindfulness incorporates all happenings that are supposed to move us on to what is meant to happen. The purpose of mindfulness is to be clear about the destiny of what is happening out in the world, and what is meant to be. Knowing the Earth's destiny gives you an accurate purpose that you know is right in your mindful consciousness. Eternity is present in your mind so you can release the past and the future and be in the only one present. The NOW is the best source energy, as it has the power to do the next job you have to do, since it is always in the now. Our thoughts are therefore always in the now, and this helps us as we move ahead, as we understand what is in the future present (the next now moment).

The past and the future is always in the present now, and the way to understand the now is through mindfulness, and until this is clear to you, you will find that mindfulness will not keep you in the now, and you will not know what to do next, to progress.

Having peace is the future 'now', and we can achieve peace, altogether, in a correct and suitable way. Meditation totally clears every future prospect from your mind, giving you a clear sense of how to maintain your wellbeing. Your gut intuition works better when you have wellbeing.

Making you the most perfect human being is an arranged composition of your different aspects to create an individual reality for yourself, that is also connected with the rest of the world. The purpose of your focused thinking is to figure out the best course of action to fulfil your goals; going onward this opens things up to ensure the highest level of guaranteed achievement that is possible. It is possible, by understanding your mind and how it works, to perform the most beautiful possibility of all that you are capable of. We can understand how everything works as we see it being compiled.

Mindful thinking develops the brain, as this is necessary for us to be able to have connection and companionship. Mindfulness is the counterpart that is the basis for a new outcome and makes it possible. It brings together a sequence of development that connects everything known together. The mindful way is to develop mindfulness in every action you take, that you have to account for. Taking positive mindful actions leads to a better outcome.

The mindfulness community will develop and spread into neighbouring communities, via the ping-pong effect of quickly passing information backwards and forwards, clarifying the benefits of mindfulness. It is always better for people to have an open mind about what is ahead of them, with the world peace that follows on after their own essence has peace. Mindfulness is remarkable as it is actualising stronger minds within us here in the material world to do the things we have to do.

The domino effect causes everyone to fulfill their purpose when they are coming together for the superior extravaganza created by mindfulness. When inner peace prevails amongst everyone, we will realise we have the mindfulness of peace. Our minds have the ability to do anything. This controls the mind so that it is mindful in consciousness on every subject that is referred to. The procedure of mindfulness is easier when you get to where you are going, and then you can continue forward by calculating how to do your next step. It is easy when you figure out what to do next and how to do it, as you make progress and it benefits your wellbeing.

A program of using mindfulness delivers the most surprising outcome. We are capable of spilling out garbage from within ourselves, and the Earth plane itself is capable of spilling out garbage through natural disasters. We are then uplifted within ourselves, and the universal energy is also uplifted, as it dissolves all confusion.

The mindfulness state is best with relaxed meditation, that can also be a guided meditation, so that our mind's eye makes continuing progress. A mindful state of excitement is great for your wellbeing, as everything comes together and flows out properly, as you are being true to your purpose. You receive enjoyment from mindfulness, as you are calm, and you have the ability to connect with joy and have a joyful frame of mind.

Without mindfulness benefits received through meditation, some people would wonder what their true destiny is. Readers of these chapters will now know the world's destiny from my explanations, but how will people know their personal destiny without mindful meditation.

The explanation will come suddenly and be controversial, as part of the sudden changes that are happening to everybody. This allows the meditation process to be performed with excitement, as it becomes more necessary and acceptable to figure out the way forward to our own destiny and the world's destiny. Moving forward with mindfulness involves the gathering of us all in one great outcome. Mindfulness will play out the way it is meant to.

Through mindfulness we will learn about eternity and everlasting life, and that there is only one present. There are always different things happening in the present. However, because there is only one present, everything is happening at once. Mindfulness meditation will be good for bringing us all through to world peace. We must be cautious and observant and realise that we have to solve the ongoing wars and conflicts.

People are being led to meditative practices through word of mouth as they hear about its benefits. This equalises things for all those who want to learn, and they figure out that they learn better when they need it, as it is necessary throughout all the communities as a whole.

The mixture and combining of all the different people with different ideas and ways of living, and different places to perform meditation, will be worthwhile. We need mindfulness meditation to uplift our minds and to have the awareness to unite for a cool collective outcome, that benefits us all. Joining together in meditation groups and classes benefits our collective wellbeing, as mindfulness has the ability to resonate with excitement.

Before we can take action, we must identify what needs to be done.

In every country we will unite as one, as all nations come together and are recognised as one collective whole.

Everything we learn in oneness education combines with what we have learnt in mindfulness, to create a calmer polite way of being, going forward. Without mindfulness, and the clear mind it gives us, we would stay behind in the third and fourth-dimensional realities, as it would be impossible to move further up. Mindfulness meditation takes you on a journey that is unforgettable, with your imagination creating your reality that comes into real life.

The fact is that we can actually change things in the world. Once we change things with our mindful way of thinking, we can slip out of unusual ways of behaving, from the old third and fourth dimensions, that others do not understand.

Every now moment is the moment to live in, and keep living in, for eternity, with love, through all our lifetimes. We will understand the full eternal connection, which is everything that exists and always has existed. There is no beginning and there is no end. There is only one eternal present that is everlasting no matter how long we go on. The way forward is just the eternal moment that is still that one same present. There is no ending as everything is everlasting. There is always something happening in the present, which is now.

The eternal everlasting presence is providing support for mindfulness. This wakes you up to what is awakening everyone else who is being helped to understand. The universe is eternal with its presence that has no judgement in any way. You can escape worry when you grasp that reality is eternal in the present.

As our spirit connects to the present and never dies, either in the material world or spiritual world, we need the understanding of this to be stable and balanced. The ongoing mindfulness of eternity beckons us with its welcoming warmth, so that we will know what our life is about and what we should do with it. Being in mindfulness meditation, we will understand clearly what is best for our wellbeing that we need to know about.

Mindfulness is connected to reality through meditation, so that we are aware that our thoughts are aligned with what is happening in our mind. Our thoughts have to be aligned with our mind to create our reality.

The more repeated thoughts we have of what we want to create, the more we can control our reality, as each one of our single thoughts builds up into mass energy.

By moving up into the fifth dimension, communication will be telepathic as there will be an absence of fear. Telepathy will be accepted, and we will communicate well and clearly.

We are developing control of our fearful thoughts so we will not have phobias. Governments and communities will help us with security to keep us safe.

Our thoughts will play out with mindfulness and make our psychic abilities more noticeable so we can communicate telepathically. We strongly recognise the advantages of meditation in developing telepathy through mindful abilities. As a result of mindfulness, we will develop telepathic communication. Momentum is strong through meditation, which gives us our gut intuition for releasing our psychic abilities, that will be applied to communicate telepathically.

We need our trusted psychic abilities to keep us on track doing what is best. Having clear mindfulness is the better way of supporting your sixth sense. You can apply this by being mindful about your health and in your daily tasks. It is crucial to be mindful in your daily life, since without mindfulness we would not have large scale peace, as we would not have inner peace. To keep your thoughts clear, release every fearful thought with continuous laughter, that leaves only love residing inside you.

Releasing fear is when the mind is clear, and then there is no danger of fear blocking your creative thinking and holding you back. You need to be moving ahead in the present moment that is now impacting you, with backup support from mindfulness and from other people in the communities.

CHAPTER 21

THE ARRIVAL

The arrival of worldwide peace will be the most extraordinary completion of the world's destiny.

My own essence is to learn and give eternal peace, and this, combined with the universal essence, completes the puzzle for world peace, with the pieces matching up and fitting into place.

It will be done by finding solutions for all the topics in the chapters of this book, and connecting them, so that all the different pieces of the puzzle from each topic will fit into place for world peace. We will have proof of heaven to give us comfort, as we make progress with the topics (in these chapters) that will change people's attitudes. The numbers will give proof of heaven, as they will add up to the correct alignment with the universe, to fulfill everything effectively to make the puzzle. We need to be aligned with the substance (matter) that is essential, with science and spirituality, so that we can prove that world peace is necessary, and we have to stay together and never give up.

The numbers speak for themselves, as follows: Number 1 means beginning. Number 5 means change. Putting these two numbers together is 15, which applies here in our material world. Both of the single digits 1 and 5 put together has significant meaning for what is taking place in the material world.

1+2+3+4+5=15
This is the numbers 1 to 5 added together. This proves that the calculation equals the same number itself, but not only that, it also proves that time is travelling three times faster in the material world.

We have proven that the material world is 15, and now we will look at number 69. This has two single numbers put together with digits that add up to exactly the same number that our material world has: 6+9=15.
We will develop these numbers more by looking inside them.
6+7+8+9=30 (adding the single digits from 6 to 9).

Now, if we add the number 30 with the number needed to equal 69 again:
30+39=69 (the number 39 is needed to be added to 30 to total 69). Number 39 will be a ladder of enlightenment to climb, right onto the bridge of the two worlds connecting.

Number 54 has great meaning for a bridge connecting both worlds. 15+54=69 (15 = material world, 54 = bridge, 69 = spiritual world).

Now we will look at number 39 again:

15+39=54 (15 = material world, 54 = bridge, 39 = ladder of enlightenment to climb onto bridge).

69+39=108

Number 108 means wholeness and completion. We will look at the material world and the spiritual world.

1+5+1+6+1+7+1+8=30 (numbers 15 to 18 added in single digits). 15 = material world, 18 = more spiritual number. 30 is the exact number of the spiritual world, with all numbers of 69 added up: 6+7+8+9=30. Number 18 is more of a spiritual number, with 1 meaning beginning, and 8 meaning achievement.

It also reflects to number 36:

1+2+3+4+5+6+7+8=36 (Numbers 1 to 8 added together).

Now we see number 36 reflecting back, (by adding the single digits from 3 to 6): 3+4+5+6=18

Taking a look now at how to get number 54:

36 (reflects from 18) + 18 (beginning achievement) = 54 (the bridge).

We can see the spiritual bond with 18 has now tripled to 54.

Now we will explore more facts about numbers and how they add up. Let us go from being at 15, to being at 18.

1+5+1+6+1+7+1+8=30 (adding 15 to 18 in single digits). Numbers have spoken with their meanings!

Looking at these numbers gives us proof that everything will happen three times better, easier and quicker, to achieve world peace. With these numbers added up and put together, we can conclude that it will seem like a miracle when we have proof of heaven, and going on further, proving the oneness connection with number 108.

How do we get onto the bridgeway to see proof of heaven? Number 15 in the material world needs to be added to another number to total 54 to get onto this bridge. 15+39=54. Number 39 is the exact number connecting the material world to the bridgeway. The number 39 means enlightenment, therefore all of humanity will look for more meaning in the lives they live.

If you see a rainbow on the bridge, it is a good sign for you, encouraging you towards Aquarius. We will understand that the bridgeway can be lengthened and have thorough proof of the oneness connection. 54x2=108. Number 54 doubled in length equals 108. This represents superpower for number 54.

These numbers will be in the computer network to prove the connection between science and spirituality. The computer network will have the information about worldwide peace and how to achieve it with the number 54 superpower: 54=18x3 (beginning and achievement), 54x2=108 (lengthens), 15+39=54 (bridge).

The connection between science and spirituality, including information from this book, will be logical and have a forceful energetic attraction in the way it appears. Being in the computer network will give it an enormous effect.

It seems as if the numbers are changing, not just in their adding up and how they speak for themselves, but also in the different way they are interpreted.

Further to this, we will add the numbers of the 21 chapters in this book. Adding the numbers from 1 to 21 in single digits: 1+2+3+4+5 (=15) +6+7+8+9+1+0+11+1+2+1+3+1+4 (=69) +1+6+1+7+1+8+1+9+2+0+2+1 = 108. Wholeness and completion. (1+5 is omitted). Master number 11 is not reduced to single digits.

I left out number 15 (1+5) from the above calculation totalling 108, as the material world already equals 15, and time and matter, having the mass evolution, is travelling three times faster than what we originally thought.

This proves a full universe of interconnectedness, as explained in this book, and all the numbers have spoken for themselves as their meaning is to confirm worldwide peace.

www.ingramcontent.com/pod-product-compliance
Lightning Source LLC
Chambersburg PA
CBHW061755290426
44109CB00030B/2868